Explorations

Intermediate
Differentiated Curriculum

Grade Levels:
4th – 6th

Length of Time:
40+ hours

ISBN 978-1-59363-283-0
© 2008 Prufrock Press Inc.

similarities and differences between
© Prufrock Press Inc.

Prufrock Press' Differentiated Curriculum Kits provide hands-on, discovery-based, research-oriented activities that are cross-curricular. Prufrock curriculum guides save valuable time, are easy to use, and are highly effective. Each unit begins with a pre-assessment and ends with a post-assessment, so growth and progress can be tracked. Lessons are tied to National and Texas State Standards, freeing teachers to spend more time with students. Each activity is a complete lesson with a focus, closure, extension(s), and suggested assessment opportunities. Differentiated strategies are also identified in every lesson. The evaluation tools are authentic, requiring students to demonstrate knowledge by practical application. Rubrics are provided to help with assessment.

We recognize that one activity cannot reach every student at every ability level, so suggestions are given for modifications. Please feel free to modify activities as needed.

Prufrock curricula are based on conceptual themes. By using abstract words such as *wonders, changes, structures*, and *powers*, the topics are broad, universal, and timeless. Research proves that conceptual learning helps bridge the disciplines requiring higher-order thinking, which in turn leads to meaningful understanding.

Come explore the world of Explorations...

We have a natural curiosity to explore our world. From the mysterious depths of the ocean to Mars, students will be challenged to go a step beyond the explorers who came before them. Social inequality and the effects of nutritional habits on the heart will be examined. Students will discover winter survival tactics and retrace the steps of some famous explorers such as Marco Polo. Alternative sources of energy, logic, cultural borrowing and the effects of ancient inventions on today's society will be investigated. Students will discover a new world of explorations waiting for them.

Acknowledgements

We would like to credit Sandra N. Kaplan, Javits Projects, University of Southern California, for the use of the Depth and Complexity Dimensions in our materials.

A special thank you to Suzy Hagar, Executive Director for Advanced Academic Services in the Carrollton-Farmers Branch Independent School District, for project development advice, suggestions, and support.

Written by: Debbie Keiser, Brenda McGee, Mary Hennenfent, and Chuck Nusinov
Cover Art by: Brandon Bolt
Edited by: Debbie Keiser, Brenda McGee, and Linda Triska

NOTE

The Web sites in this curriculum were working and age-appropriate at the time of publication, but Prufrock Press Inc. has no control over any subsequent changes.

Table of Contents

Planning Materials   **Page**

Unit Planner and Overview   7
Enduring Understandings and Generalizations   8
Guiding Questions   9

Activities

1. Pre-Assessment   11
2. The Path of Marco Polo   13
3. Civilized or Not?   17
4. Cultural Borrowing   19
5. Space Exploration   21
6. Puzzles of the World   24
7. Exploring the Ocean Floor   28
8. Explore Your Nutritional Habits   31
9. Hunger in America   34
10. When Did It Happen?   36
11. Ancient Inventions   38
12. Exploring the Impossible   40
13. The Greatest Explorers   43
14. Winter Survival   45
15. Exploring Energy   47
16. Geometric Explorations   50
17. Post-Assessment   52

Attachments

1. Journal Assembly   53
2. Time Traveling Logic Problem   55
3. Blank Evaluation Rubric   56
4. Guessing Game Words   57
5. Cultural Borrowing   58
6. Learning Loop   59
7. Generalization Rubric   61
8. Evaluation Rubric   62
9. Scientific Method   63
10. Pangaea Jigsaw   64
11. World Map   65
12. News Flash!   66
13. Brochure Evaluation   67
14. Explorer Tic-Tac-Toe   68

Attachments

		Page
15.	Six Hat Thinking	69
16.	Paper Pyramids	71

Checklists

Vocabulary and Materials	72
Differentiation Strategies and TEKS	74
National Standards	86

Notes

_____

_____

_____

_____

_____

_____

_____

_____

_____

_____

_____

_____

_____

_____

_____

_____

_____

_____

_____

_____

_____

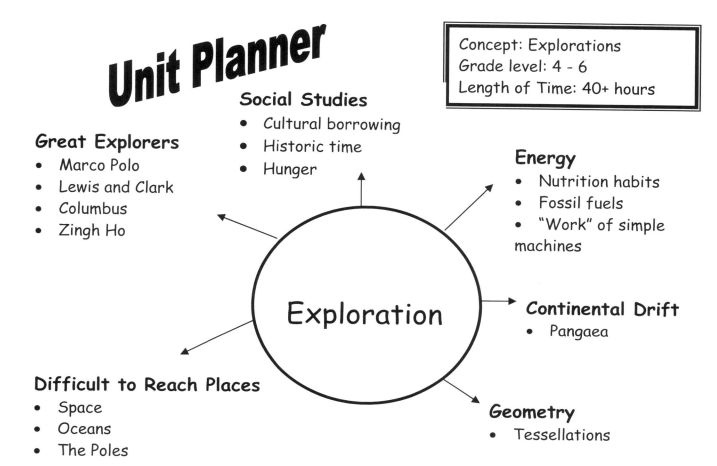

Unit Planner

Concept: Explorations
Grade level: 4 - 6
Length of Time: 40+ hours

Social Studies
- Cultural borrowing
- Historic time
- Hunger

Great Explorers
- Marco Polo
- Lewis and Clark
- Columbus
- Zingh Ho

Energy
- Nutrition habits
- Fossil fuels
- "Work" of simple machines

Exploration

Continental Drift
- Pangaea

Difficult to Reach Places
- Space
- Oceans
- The Poles

Geometry
- Tessellations

Unit Overview

In the Explorations curriculum, students will be challenged to go a step beyond the explorers who came before them. Social inequality and the effects of nutritional habits on the heart will be examined. Students will discover winter survival tactics and retrace the steps of some famous explorers such as Marco Polo. Alternative sources of energy, logic, and the effects of ancient inventions on today's society will be investigated. Students will discover a new world of explorations waiting for them.

Enduring Understandings and Generalizations

The travels of explorers may influence history.

Explorers may transfer parts of their culture to other cultures.

The explorations of new frontiers may impact advancements in other fields of study.

Exploring societal issues, such as hunger and energy sources, may promote solutions to these problems.

Perseverance may make previously impossible tasks a reality.

Accomplishing previously impossible tasks may encourage future explorers to take a calculated risk.

Guiding Questions for *Explorations*

Guiding questions are the factual (F), conceptual (C), and philosophical (P) questions addressed in the curriculum. These are the questions students should be able to answer after completing the activities in this curriculum.

(F) What things can be explored?
(F) Who was Marco Polo?
(F) What is a culture?
(F) What is civilization?
(F) What is cultural borrowing?
(F) Who was Robert Goddard?
(F) What is the theory of continental drift?
(F) What evidence exists to support the continental drift theory?
(F) What is a submersible?
(F) What are the nutritional requirements for each body system?
(F) What is meant by a Third World Country?
(F) How long have people inhabited the Earth?
(F) What is the force called work?
(F) What are the types of simple machines?
(F) What is perseverance?
(F) What accomplishments were once believed impossible?
(F) Who were some of the greatest explorers?
(F) What are the three basic needs for survival?
(F) What are fossil fuels?
(F) What are some examples of alternate forms of energy?
(F) What are tessellations?

(C) How did Marco Polo's travels influence history?
(C) Why do cultures tend to borrow from one another?
(C) How did the individual events of space exploration influence other fields of study?
(C) How did the theory of continental drift revolutionize geology?
(C) How has technology improved the ability of humans to explore the oceans?
(C) Why is it necessary for all body systems to function properly?
(C) Why are there people who go hungry in the United States?
(C) How can you make a scale time line of an historical period?
(C) How do simple machines make work easier?
(C) How have the achievements of explorers who persevered to accomplish the impossible changed our reality?
(C) How did the contributions of great explorers affect society?
(C) How does Brian accomplish his survival needs?
(C) Why would an all meat diet be lacking in nutrition?

(C) How do patterns differ between cultures?

(C) Why did people create tessellations?

(P) Should we continue to explore space?

(P) Should the government be responsible for helping those who are hungry in America?

(P) Should the American government help resolve the hunger problem in foreign countries when there are problems in America?

F= factual question

C= conceptual question

P= philosophical question

Notes

_____

_____

_____

_____

_____

_____

_____

_____

_____

_____

_____

_____

_____

Activity 1 - Pre-Assessment

Differentiation Strategies
Knowledge and Skills
- Attributes
- Classifying

Innovation and Application
- Fluency
- Flexibility

Multiple Perspectives
- Shared Inquiry
- Brainstorming

Instructional Materials
- 5 blank transparencies
- overhead projector
- 5 dry-erase markers
- journals

A. Write the word *Explorations* on the chalkboard. Challenge students to brainstorm and record all the things that can be explored. (They can use existing journals, spiral notebooks or create one using Attachment 1.) After 2 minutes of quiet, individual work, have students draw a line below the last brainstormed item.

B. Have teams of four discuss their lists. Allow 2 minutes for discussion, then 5 minutes for students to add to their lists.

C. Invite students to share with the group all the things that can be explored. Record the items on the chalkboard.

D. Have students form five teams. Provide each team with a transparency and dry-erase marker. Challenge teams to create a word web that categorizes the list on the chalkboard. See example on the next page. Encourage students to develop their own categories.

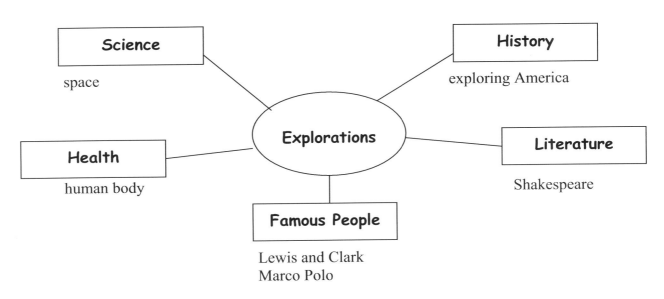

E. Have each team develop a presentation using the transparency as a visual.

F. After teams categorize the list, invite them to present their graphic organizers to the class. Encourage teams to discuss how they selected the categories and separated the topics.

G. Keep the original papers and the transparencies from the presentations for comparison after the Post-Assessment.

Notes

_____

_____

_____

_____

_____

_____

_____

_____

_____

_____

_____

Activity 2 - The Path of Marco Polo

Differentiation Strategies

Knowledge and Skills
- Visualization
- Research

Analysis and Synthesis
- Evaluate Situations
- Draw Conclusions
- SCAMPER

Relevance and Significance
- Group Consensus
- Field Lesson

Enduring Understanding
Explorers may transfer parts of their culture to other cultures.

Guiding Questions
(F) What things can be explored?
(F) Who was Marco Polo?

Instructional Materials
- multiple matching copies of *Marco Polo: A Journey Through China* book, by Fiona MacDonald
- atlas and/or globe
- butcher paper, construction paper, and markers
- copies of Attachment 2

Background Information

Marco Polo (1254-1324) was the first European to cross Asia and leave a record of what he saw and heard while exploring the continent.

Polo was born in Venice, Italy. His mother died shortly thereafter, and his father saw him for the first time when he was 15 years old. Marco Polo was raised by his aunts and uncles.

Polo's father and uncle were Venetian merchants and business partners. When they finally returned to Venice to see the family, they were on a **mission** for the Mongolian emperor Kublai Khan. They stayed in Venice for two years before continuing on their mission and their final destination, China. Polo, at age 17, joined them.

Marco Polo entered Kublai Khan's diplomatic service, acting as his agent on missions to many parts of the empire and serving as a governor for three years. The Polos stayed in China until 1292. Then they left to escort a Mongol princess traveling to Iran. They arrived in Venice in 1295.

Marco Polo was taken prisoner in 1298 when he was captain of a Venetian galley that participated in a battle between the fleets of Venice and Genoa. During his imprisonment in Genoa, he dictated the detailed account of his travels to a fellow prisoner. He was released in 1299 and returned to Venice.

Marco Polo's story, *The Travels of Marco Polo*, is the most famous and influential travel book in history. It has a wealth of vivid detail and gave medieval Europe its first real knowledge of China and other Asian countries, including Thailand, Japan, Java, Vietnam, Sri Lanka, Tibet, India, and Burma. For a long time it was the only source in Europe for information on the geography and life in the Far East. The book became the basis for some of Europe's first accurate maps of Asia. It helped to arouse Christopher Columbus' interest in the Orient, which culminated in his discovery of America in 1492 while attempting to reach the Far East. He took a copy of Marco Polo's book on his voyage.

A. Share the Background Information and discuss whether Polo's childhood was typical of today or unique to the times. Discuss what effect Polo's early childhood, without his parents, could have had on his development.

B. Have students read in pairs if multiple copies of *Marco Polo: A Journey Through China* are available. If this is not possible, have students take turns reading aloud, or read the book to the class.

C. Challenge students to record locations where Marco Polo traveled.

D. Guide students through a SCAMPER experience. You may choose to make copies of the next page if you like.

Teacher Tip
SCAMPER can be used to help students develop new thoughts and ideas and aids the creative thinking process. SCAMPER is an acronym for: **s**ubstitute, **c**ombine, **a**dapt, **m**odify/**m**agnify/**m**inify, **p**ut to other uses, **e**liminate, **r**everse/rearrange.

S: Substitute
What do you think might have happened if Marco Polo had been raised by his parents instead of his aunts and uncles?

C: Combine
What might have happened if Marco Polo had been afraid of the ocean and been raised by a wealthy merchant?

A: Adapt
How might the story have changed if Marco Polo had had a younger brother or sister to look after while he was growing up?

M: Modify
What might have happened if Marco Polo's first voyage had ended in complete failure?

P: Put to other uses
What if Marco had only been interested in exploration so he could become wealthy?

E: Eliminate a feature of the story
How might the story of Marco Polo have changed if he had not been imprisoned and written his book?

R: Rearrange or reverse the sequence of the story.
How would the story of Marco Polo's exploration change if Marco Polo had been born a girl?

E. Ask students to work as partners to draw a map of the **Eastern Hemisphere**. Have them make symbols to attach to the map at various points that illustrate what Marco Polo found or experienced there. For example, a tiny prison cell could be the symbol in Genoa.

Closure
Instruct students to draw a line, tiny footprints, or other directional marks on the map to trace Polo's travels.

Extensions
A. Have students create a skit or play that illustrates Marco Polo's travels.

B. Ask students to complete the Time Traveling Logic Problem on Attachment 2.

C. Have students create their own logic problem following the example on Attachment 2.

D. Invite students to use a map, atlas, or globe to estimate the distance Marco Polo traveled between destinations.

Assessment
Check for the accuracy of the route on the map.

Notes

Activity 3 - Civilized or Not?

Differentiation Strategies
Knowledge and Skills
- Etymology
- Classifying

Innovation and Application
- Flexibility
- Fluency

Multiple Perspectives
- Shared inquiry
- Brainstorming

Instructional Materials
- journals
- computer with Internet access

Enduring Understanding
Explorers may transfer parts of their culture to other cultures.

Guiding Questions
(F) What is a culture?
(F) What is civilization?

Background Information
Culture is part of every person's life. It is everything a person believes, learns, and does as a member of a specific group. Culture is affected by a variety of things including environment, technology, and social interaction.

Once a culture has reached a certain level (advanced in social organization and the arts and sciences, cultured and courteous and refined) it is considered **civilized** and a **civilization**.

A. Tell students that Marco Polo traveled through many cultures as he explored the world. Have students brainstorm to define culture. (Share the Background Information.)

B. Ask students to discuss clues people might use to identify them as Americans in a foreign country.

C. Ask students to brainstorm and record the cultural aspects they would carry with them if they moved to another country. (Food, recreation, shared ideas or beliefs, customs, traditions, tools, types of government, shelter, family structure, educational opportunities, careers, arts, languages, religions, clothing styles, etc.)

D. Ask students what cultural aspects they would gladly give up if they moved to another country. Have them record their answers in their journal.

Closure

Have students work in small groups to create a list of evidence that would prove that America is a civilized country. Before students begin the project have them develop a scoring rubric using the blank rubric on Attachment 3.

Extensions

A. Ask students to find pictures in magazines that reflect their culture. Have them create a cultural collage.

Note

The Web sites in this curriculum were working and age-appropriate at the time of publication, but Prufrock Press has no control over any subsequent changes.

> **Teacher Tip**
> Rubrics are an effective assessment tool in evaluating student performance in areas that are complex and vague. By involving students in the creation of the rubric, the students take more responsibility for their own learning.

B. Allow students to explore the differences in mathematics of various cultures. Students can be introduced to topics such as: Babylonians, Egyptians, Greek, Indian, Arabic and Mayan Mathematics. An excellent web site for this exploration is:
http://www-gap.dcs.st-and.ac.uk/~history/Indexes/HistoryTopics.html

Assessment

Have students assess the Closure activity using the rubric they developed.

Notes

Activity 4 – Cultural Borrowing

Differentiation Strategies
Knowledge and Skills
- Etymology
- Research

Innovation and Application
- Logic Problems
- Fluency

Analysis and Synthesis
- Generalizations
- Inferences

Instructional Materials
- 1 copy of Attachment 4
- 6 copies of Attachment 5
- 1 copy of Attachment 6
- index cards
- tape

Enduring Understanding
Explorers may transfer parts of their culture to other cultures.

Guiding Questions
(F) What is cultural borrowing?
(C) Why do cultures tend to borrow from one another?

Preparation
Cut apart the words on Attachment 4. Tape each word to an index card. Turn the cards over so students can not see what is on the card.

Background Information
Every culture borrows components from other cultures. This is referred to as **cultural borrowing**. One famous example of this is Marco Polo bringing spaghetti from China to Italy, then spaghetti becoming one of Italy's most popular dishes.

A. Tell students that cultural borrowing began with explorers. One example is the corn tortilla, a typical Spanish food that is now popular in many cultures. Café is a word in English that describes a small restaurant, but it is really a French word. Black eyeliner is popular in many countries, but it originated in ancient Egypt, where both men and women wore it to protect their eyes from the sun, sand, and insects. It was also a beauty enhancer.

B. Ask a volunteer to be first to play a guessing game. Bring that student to the front of the room. Tape one of the index cards on the student's back. Ask the student to turn around so all the other students can see the word.

C. Tell the volunteer that the word taped to his or her back is a word that is something we "borrowed" from another culture years ago. Tell the volunteer he or she can only ask 21 yes/no questions to determine the word. The only hint is that the word is either an object, an activity or sport, or a type of system. Have one student record the number of questions asked. After the 21 questions, have students give the volunteer clues so the word can be guessed.

D. Select another player and continue the game.

E. Have students complete the cultural borrowing matrix on Attachment 5.

F. Have students participate in the Learning Loop on Attachment 6. The person with the smiley face on his/her card should read their card first. Play continues until all cards have been read and answers loop back to the beginning.

G. Help students write generalizations about culture, civilization, and cultural borrowing. Use the rubric on Attachment 7 as your guide in evaluating the results. Some examples might be:
• Civilized countries have strong forms of government.
• An object that is generally assumed to have originated in one country may have been "borrowed" from another.

Closure
Have students write a paragraph summarizing what they have learned about cultural borrowing then have them read aloud what they wrote.

Extensions
A. Explain that **etymology** is the study of the origin and development of a word; tracing a word back as far as possible. Have students explore the following Web sites and report words which most interested or surprised them. As always, please preview all sites before allowing student access.
http://library.thinkquest.org/5585/rootwords.htm
http://spanish.about.com/cs/historyofspanish/a/spanishloanword.htm
http://www.ruf.rice.edu/~kemmer/Words/loanwords.html

B. Have students work with a small group to brainstorm then illustrate more examples of cultural borrowing.

Assessment
Use the rubric on Attachment 8 to assess the paragraph from the Closure activity.

Activity 5 - Space Exploration

Differentiation Strategies
Analysis and Synthesis
- Creative Problem Solving
- Generalizations

Ethics/Unanswered Questions
- Provocative Questions
- Problem Defining

Multiple Perspectives
- Evaluate Situations
- Shared Inquiry

Methodology and Use of Resources
- Research

Instructional Materials
- computer with Internet access
- books about space exploration

Enduring Understanding
The explorations of new frontiers may impact advancements in other fields of study.

Guiding Questions
(F) Who was Robert Goddard?
(C) How did the individual events of space exploration influence other fields of study?
(P) Should we continue to explore space?

Background Information
For centuries people have wondered about space. The Mayans, Egyptians, Chinese, and other **ancient** cultures plotted the movements of the moon and stars and developed calendars based on them. **Galileo** invented the telescope to get a closer look at the moon and planets in our solar system.

As technology became more advanced, steam engines then fuel engines were created, and some people became curious about space travel. **Robert Goddard** (1882–1945) built the first rocket and is considered the "father of the Space Age." By the end of his life, scientists were already working on a way to send people into space.

In 1957, the Soviet Union became the first country to put a **satellite** into space. Thus began the space race between the Soviets and the United States. The goal soon changed from simply going into space to landing on the moon. On July 20, 1969, Americans Neil Armstrong and Buzz Aldrin landed on the moon, becoming the first people to touch down on an object in outer space.

Development of the space shuttle allowed multiple space missions using the same craft. NASA will continue to explore space with the Hubble Telescope until no longer active.

NASA will use the James Webb Space Telescope starting in 2011, and traveling space probes will continue to gather data about the known planets in our solar system.

A. Tell students there was a time when people wondered if anyone would set foot on the moon. Ask students what they wonder about space travel. (Possible responses include: Will people travel to Mars? Are there life forms on other planets?)

B. Invite teams to research the history of space exploration using the books provided and the Web site below. As always, please preview all sites before allowing student access. **http://adc.gsfc.nasa.gov/adc/education/space_ex/index.html**

C. Have teams create time lines of space exploration. Invite students to share their findings and combine all research into one large time line.

D. Ask students to consider the following questions:
- What technological advances led to people walking on the moon?
- How do you think other fields of study, such as literature and medicine, were affected by the space race?
- Based on the advances in space travel over the past 50 years, what leaps in space exploration do you predict in the next 50 years? 75 years? 100 years?
- How are traveling in space and exploring the bottom of the ocean alike?
- What country has been the most successful in space exploration? Provide references to support your answers.
- What should be the protocol if an astronaut ever encounters an alien? Should we capture and examine the being, as we do with newly discovered animals, insects, and plants? Or should we try to communicate? What steps should be taken to ensure our safety and the safety of aliens?
- Can you think of any reasons people might be against space exploration? Consider for a moment that you belong to a group that does not support space exploration. What reasons would your group give to persuade others to think as you do?

E. Share the rubric on Attachment 8 or create your own rubric using Attachment 3. Explain the criteria to earn a top score for a research project and presentation.

F. Have students form small teams to research one of the questions about space exploration. Ask teams to compile their research into informative essays to be presented orally.

G. Have students write generalizations about space exploration or space explorers. Use the Rubric on Attachment 7 for assessment.

Closure
Invite students to present their essays to the class. Initiate a brainstorming session about things we still do not know or understand about space.

Extensions

A. Encourage students to research the distance to each of the inner planets (Mercury, Venus, and Mars) in miles. Ask students to determine the fastest time a manned space shuttle could travel in miles per hour. Have students calculate the time it would take to reach each planet from Earth. Have students discuss the likelihood of traveling to another planet using current technology. Ask students to investigate the use of scientific notation to assist in the recording of these distances. Ask: How can scientific notation be useful to the space traveler?

B. Tell students that many scientists believe we will put a person on Mars by 2020. Ask students to brainstorm the challenges scientists will face to do this. Have students go to the following Web sites to discover the plans that are being discussed to make the trip to Mars a reality. As always, please preview any site before allowing student access.
http://mars.jpl.nasa.gov/
http://www.marsacademy.com/

C. Obtain permission from your principal to create a Web site highlighting student research. You may need to enlist the help of the technology specialist. Have students help plan and design the site. They should create a site map on paper showing the links.

Assessment

Use the rubric on Attachment 8 or the one that students created from a blank rubric to evaluate student presentations.

Notes

_____

_____

_____

_____

_____

_____

_____

_____

_____

_____

_____

Activity 6 – Puzzles of the World

Differentiation Strategies
Knowledge and Skills
- Research
- Demonstration

Analysis and Synthesis
- Convergent and Divergent Thinking
- Problem Defining

Multiple Perspectives
- Evaluate Situations
- Transformation

Relevance and Significance
- Group Consensus
- Field Lesson

Instructional Materials
- 3 copies of Attachment 9 (Scientific Method)
- 3 copies of Attachment 10 (Pangaea Jigsaw)
- 3 copies of Attachment 11 (World Map)
- 3 copies of Attachment 12 (News Flash!)
- computer with Internet access

Enduring Understanding
The explorations of new frontiers may impact advancements in other fields of study.

Guiding Questions
(F) What is the theory of continental drift?
(F) What evidence exists to support the continental drift theory?
(C) How did the theory of continental drift revolutionize geology?

Background
Alfred Wegener (1880–1930) studied to be an astronomer but decided to work in the fields of **climatology** (the study of climates around the world) and **meteorology** (the study of weather). In 1915, Wegener proposed the theory of **continental drift**, the idea that the continents are in motion. Wegener studied maps and hypothesized that all the continents were once connected as one **supercontinent** later named **Pangaea**. Scientists disagreed with Wegener's theories at the time, but Wegener caused a **revolution** in the study of geology. Soon discoveries were made that began to prove his theory. Similar rock formations, fossils of reptiles, and fossils of ferns were found on the coasts of southwest Africa and in South America. Another exciting development was the

discovery of dinosaur fossils under the ice of Antarctica. Scientists believe dinosaurs were reptiles and lived in warm, wet climates, suggesting that Antarctica was once warm and wet. It was not until 1960 that Wegener's theories were accepted by most of the science community.

Preparation

Cut apart each puzzle on Attachment 10 and place them in three designated lab areas. Place copies of Attachment 11 with the puzzles.

A. Direct students to three lab groups. Distribute copies of Attachment 9 and invite students to read the page aloud. Tell students that the following evidence has been left for them to study. They are to examine the evidence (the puzzle and world map) and use the scientific method to draw conclusions about the evidence.

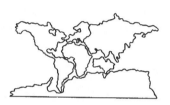

B. If students are having trouble, tell them some scientists believe that millions of years ago the continents were once connected like a giant puzzle. Have students label the continents, then piece the puzzle together as it may have looked millions of years ago. Allow 15-20 minutes for students to study the evidence. Ask one person in each group to record their observations about the evidence. Then ask students to formulate questions about their observations. Have students share observations and questions with the class.

Sample observations:
- The pieces of the puzzle look like the continents on the world map.
- The pieces of the puzzle do not exactly fit together.
- The coast of South America looks like it might have been a part of Africa at one time.

Sample questions:
- Why were we given this puzzle and a world map?
- How is the evidence we were given connected?
- Is it possible that all the continents were connected a long time ago?

C. Ask students to write down their predictions, or hypotheses, based on the new evidence. Ask students to determine what the information means. Have students share their ideas with the class. For guidance, ask students what they think caused the large landmass to separate into different continents. See the sample hypothesis below:

> *We predict that a long time ago the continents were joined together like a giant puzzle. We think the continents drifted apart because the mantle is liquid.*

D. Distribute copies of Attachment 12 (News Flash!) to lab groups. Tell students to read the new evidence. Have students write about how the evidence helps support their hypotheses. Then ask students to share what they wrote. See the possible answer on next page:

We thought the puzzle was like the continents as they look today. The new evidence helped us see that the continents may have been connected a long time ago. The west coast of South America and east coast of Africa have fossils of plants and animals that are the same. The coal and dinosaur fossils that were found in Antarctica helps support our hypothesis because they could not have been there forever.

E. Invite students to draw conclusions about the evidence and form a theory. Have them record their theories. See the sample theory below:

Based on the evidence, we have decided that South America, Africa, and Antarctica were joined a long time ago. All seven continents might have been joined at one time.

F. Share the Background Information. Ask students how the new evidence supports Alfred Wegener's theory. Have students record their thoughts for the Conclusion part of the scientific method.

G. Help students visit the following Web sites. As always, please preview all sites before allowing student access.
- This Web site lists games to help students learn geology vocabulary.
http://www.quia.com/custom/514main.html
- This Web site is an interactive map game that helps students identify the seven continents within Pangaea.
http://kids.earth.nasa.gov/archive/pangaea/Pangaea_game.html

Closure
A. Have students discuss why it is important to know about Pangaea. (Possible response: Pangaea helps explain how the same kind of fossils can be found on two different continents. It also helps us understand that our continents are still in motion.)

B. Tell students that Japan is about 5,200 miles from California. Researchers have determined that California moves between 1–4 inches closer to Japan each year. Ask students the below questions. (You will need to guide the thinking and help students with the multiplication. It is not important that they do the multiplication. Students should be able to tell you how the problem should be worked to get to the answer.)
- How many inches are in 1 foot? (12)
- If California moves 4 inches per year, how long would it take California to move 1 foot? (3 years)
- One mile equals 5,280 feet. About how long will it take for California to move 1 mile? (Rounding 5,280 to 5,000, it will take about 15,000 years – 5,000 feet x 3 years.)
- Japan is about 5,200 miles from California. About how many years will it take California to reach Japan? (Rounding 5,200 to 5,000, it will take about 75 million years – 5,000 miles x 15,000 years.)

Extensions
A. Have students research Alfred Wegener's life and determine the effects of his research

B. Invite students to put together a visual presentation of how Pangaea broke into seven continents. Have them make large props, such as drawings of each continent on a large piece of paper, and write a script. Then have them present a Pangaea Play to another class.

C. Invite students to go to the following Web site to learn more about Pangaea and see more video evidence that supports the Pangaea theory. As always, please preview the site before allowing student access.
http://library.thinkquest.org/17701/high/pangaea/?tqskip=1

D. Pose the following problem to students:
The continents are constantly in motion. Using one of the Web sites we visited, study the direction each continent is traveling. Can you predict where the continents will end up in millions of years? Draw a picture of your predictions

E. Challenge students to find the total square miles for all land masses on earth. Then have them calculate the fraction that each continent represents of all land. Have students convert this fraction to a percentage.

F. Have students examine populations on different continents. Which continent has the most people? Which continent has the highest population per square mile? Which has the least? Have students write generalizations based on their findings.

Assessment
Assess student understanding of continental drift and the scientific method by reading their responses.

Notes

Activity 7 - Exploring the Ocean Floor

Differentiation Strategies

Knowledge and Skills
- Research
- Drawing Conclusions

Analysis and Synthesis
- Evaluate Situations
- Classifying

Multiple Perspectives
- Inquiry
- Shared Inquiry

Communication
- Demonstration
- Writing Skills

Instructional Materials
- computer with Internet access
- books about ocean floor exploration

Enduring Understanding
The explorations of new frontiers may impact advancements in other fields of study.

Guiding Questions
(F) What is a submersible?
(C) How has technology improved the ability of humans to explore the oceans?

Background Information

Roughly 75 percent of the Earth's surface is water. People have explored every corner of our world, but the deep ocean remains a mystery to most. Special **submersibles** have been developed to help explore the ocean floor, but such exploration is very expensive.

As with space, people have been curious about what lies at the bottom of the ocean. Without special equipment, only trained divers can dive to about 100 feet below the surface safely. Then they have to resurface for air. The world record for diving is 428 feet. The person making the dive held his breath an amazing two minutes, eleven seconds.

People first chose to dive into the ocean for food and treasures to trade with one another. Later, people wanted to depend on something other than their lungs to dive beneath the waves. Edmund Halley's diving bell is one of the earliest documented diving devices. The bell took divers down to about 60 feet below the surface.

A. Share the Background Information. Initiate a discussion to see what students know about ocean research.

B. Allow students to access the following Web site to learn more about the steps humans took to explore the ocean floor centuries ago. As always, please preview the site before allowing student access.

http://seagrant.wisc.edu/madisonjason11/timeline/index_4500BC.html

C. Encourage students to choose one of the following topics to research and present a report. If students would like to use the Internet independently as a part of their research, use a filtered search engine such as www.yahooligans.com. Remember that even the best filters do not catch all questionable content, so preview sites before allowing students to view them.

- Edmund Halley and the diving bell
- Jacques Cousteau and the iron lung
- John Lethbridge and his armored diving suit
- giant tube worms at the bottom of the ocean
- deep sea vents
- the Marianas Trench
- submersibles

> **Teacher Tip**
> **Bloom's Taxonomy** of learning objectives is the easiest and one of the best ways to **differentiate**. Use your favorite search engine to find and print a chart to keep close. Move your students up the taxonomy by changing your verbs at the **Knowledge, Comprehension, Application, Analysis, Synthesis,** and **Evaluation** levels.

D. Review the evaluation rubric on Attachment 8 with students or have students create their own rubrics. Make sure students understand the criteria upon which their projects will be evaluated.

E. Encourage students to develop clever and creative ways to present the information they compile, such as creating a videotaped documentary, creating a game show, writing a song, creating an interactive Web site, or creating a collage and written report that explains why each piece in the collage helps tell about the subject.

Closure
Invite students to share their presentations.

Extensions

A. Encourage students to select an historical figure in ocean exploration about whom to write and perform a play. Students may use the research gathered by one of the teams to complete the writing of the play. Encourage students to produce props and write songs to accompany the play. You may wish to enlist the help of the music teacher.

B. Invite other classes to see the student production. Videotape the play and allow students to take the videotape home to share with their families.

C. Obtain a bag of mutli-colored goldfish crackers. Use this bag of goldfish to introduce or reinforce the concepts of probability.

D. Invite students to use tangrams to create images of marine life.

Assessment

Evaluate student projects using the rubric they selected.

Notes

Activity 8 – Explore Your Nutritional Habits

Differentiation Strategies
Knowledge and Skills
- Attributes
- Classifying

Multiple Perspectives
- Brainstorming
- Inquiry

Methodology and Use of Resources
- Research
- Shared Inquiry

Instructional Materials
- books about the human body
- computer with Internet access

Enduring Understanding
Exploring societal issues, such as hunger and energy sources, may promote solutions to these problems.

Guiding Questions
(F) What are the nutritional requirements for each body system?
(C) Why is it necessary for all body systems to function properly?
(C) Why would an all meat diet be lacking in nutrition?

Background Information
The human body is one of the most complex organisms on Earth. Our bodies work as a system. We eat when we are hungry, we sit in front of a fan to cool off, and we sleep when we are tired. These decisions are controlled by the brain and the nervous system. Each body system depends on other parts to function properly. When one part is ill, it affects the entire body **system**.

People need food, water, vitamins, and minerals for their bodies to work properly. These things, combined with exercise, proper diet, and rest, keep the body in working order.

A. Invite students to brainstorm the systems in the body (**circulatory**, **respiratory**, **excretory**, **nervous**, **digestive**, **skeletal**, and **muscular** systems). Have students name body parts within each system and list them on the chalkboard using the following sample.

Circulatory System	Respiratory System	Excretory System	Nervous System	Digestive System
heart arteries veins capillaries blood	lungs trachea diaphragm nose	kidney liver bladder	brain nerves spinal cord	mouth saliva teeth esophagus stomach large intestine small intestine

Skeletal System	Muscular System			
bones joints	muscles tendons			

B. Have students form teams of three. Challenge each team to examine the chart of body systems and parts. Have teams create cause-and-effect charts showing the relationships among various systems and parts. See the example below.

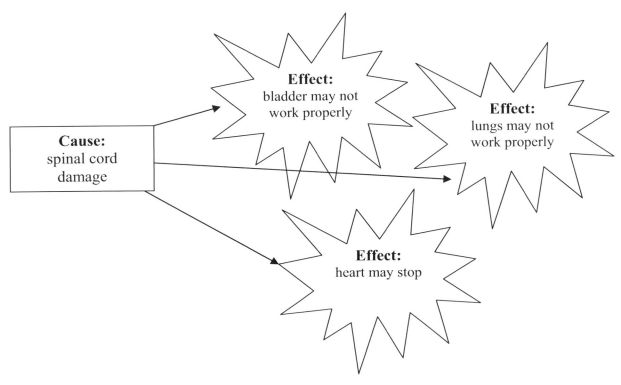

C. After students create several scenarios, have them choose one to research. Provide books and Internet access. As always, please preview Web sites before allowing student access.

D. Encourage students to find information about the nutritional requirements to keep the systems they choose healthy. For example, we need calcium for strong bones. Have students find the suggested daily requirements for these vitamins and minerals and present a chart with their research.

E. Have students create an informative brochure including the following information:
- the body system
- its function in the body
- nutritional requirements to keep it healthy
- some ways the system can be damaged or become ill
- the effects on other body systems when this system is not functioning properly
- bibliography of sources used (on the back of the brochure)

F. Review the Brochure Rubric on Attachment 13 so students will know the expectations for the project. Make changes that the students and you agree upon.

G. Help students decide how many columns they will use on their brochures. Single-, double-, and tri-fold brochures can be created using the "Columns" feature under the "Format" menu of most word processing programs on computers.

H. Have students print their completed brochures. Instruct them to draw a picture that represents the body system on the front of the brochure. Make copies of each brochure and get permission from the school nurse and librarian to display the brochures in the nurse's office and library.

Closure

Have students answer the following questions in their journals.
- What things are necessary for all body systems to function properly?
- Which body system is most important, or is one more important than another? Explain your answer.
- Can the body survive without one of its systems?

Extensions

A. Encourage students to create a class Web site showcasing their brochures and information.

B. Using the daily requirements researched in a previous activity, have students track the number of calories, fat grams and carbohydrates they eat in a day. Use the Internet to search for food lists with appropriate counts. Allow students to display their eating habits in a chart or graph. Compare the recommended daily allowances and student eating habits.

Teacher Tip

Invite a dietitian to share information about proper diet and exercise. Be sure your guest addresses the importance of proper diet for the health of each system listed.

Assessment

Assess the answers in the Closure activity. Use the rubric on Attachment 13 to evaluate the brochures.

Activity 9 - Hunger in America

Differentiation Strategies

Analysis and Synthesis
- Evaluate Situations
- Problem Sensitivity

Ethics/Unanswered Questions
- Provocative Questions
- Problem Defining

Multiple Perspectives
- Brainstorming
- Point of View

Communication
- Research

Enduring Understanding

Exploring societal issues, such as hunger and energy sources, may promote solutions to these problems.

Guiding Questions

(F) What is meant by Third World Country?
(C) Why are there people who go hungry in the United States?
(P) Should the American government help resolve the hunger problem in foreign countries when there are problems in America.

Instructional Materials
- computer with Internet access

Background Information

Many people suffer from hunger, especially those in **Third World** countries (also referred to as **Emerging Nations**) such as Honduras and Ethiopia. Our television screens burn memories into our minds of naked children sitting in the dirt with tiny arms and legs and distended stomachs from lack of food. While such pictures do not come from the United States, slightly more than 1/5 of Americans are seeking help to get enough to eat. The hunger problem is not restricted to the homeless or elderly. Many people who have at least one family member working, suffer from hunger as well.

As discussed in Activity 8, proper nutrition is important for the body to function correctly. In this activity, students will explore the causes of hunger in America, what is being done to help people, and the effects of hunger on America's children.

A. Share the first two paragraphs of the Background Information. Draw a circle on the chalkboard and divide it into five parts, then ask for a volunteer to shade in 1/5 of the circle. Ask students if they are surprised to learn that more than 1/5 of Americans suffer from hunger. Have students convert 1/5 to a percentage. Review percentages using a sample group of 100. For example, 20 percent of 100 people is 20, 40 percent of 100 people is 40, etc.

B. Have students access the following Web site. It is a study of hunger in America done in 2001. As always, please preview the site before allowing student access.
http://www.secondharvest.org/site_content.asp?s=5

C. Have students use the Web site to answer the following questions.
- What are some causes of hunger in America?
- What is being done to help hungry people in America?
- What are the effects of hunger on growing children?

D. Have students compile their findings into persuasive essays.

Closure

Invite students to share their essays with the class. Lead a class discussion about hunger in America. Ask the following questions:
- Should the government be responsible for helping those who are hungry in America? Why or why not?
- Should the American government help solve the hunger problem in foreign countries when there are problems in America? Why or why not?
- What trends do you see in hunger over the past 10 years in America? What are the causes of the trends?

Extensions

A. Encourage students to devise a campaign to educate people about hunger in America and world hunger. Help students prepare a presentation to give to the student body to raise awareness of this problem.

B. Have students write to the principal for permission to speak at a PTA meeting to raise awareness of hunger. Encourage students to get involved with organizations listed on the Web site.

C. Ask students to keep their leftovers from lunch and weigh them. Give students the opportunity to weigh all of their uneaten food items before they throw them away at lunch time. Keep a record of the wasted food and graph it daily. Challenge students to reduce the amount of food wasted at lunch. Challenge other classes to do the same and see which class can waste the least amount of food.

Assessment

Use the rubric on Attachment 8 to evaluate the essays and questions from the Closure activity.

Activity 10 - When Did It Happen?

Differentiation Strategies
Knowledge and Skills
- Attributes
- Inquiry

Analysis and Synthesis
- Evaluate Situations
- Group Consensus

Communication
- Uses Technological Media
- Demonstration

Instructional Materials
- 1 roll of toilet tissue
- marker

Enduring Understanding
The explorations of new frontiers may impact advancements in other fields of study.

Guiding Questions
(F) How long have people inhabited the Earth?
(C) How can you make a scale time line of an historical period?

Background Information
A time line lists important events within a particular historical period. About 1,500 years ago, a monk worked out a Christian system for dating events, starting with the year he believed Jesus Christ was born. He called the years after this event "anno Domini" (in the year of our Lord). This term is often referred to as **A.D.** The years before Christ's birth are "before Christ," as in 1200 **B.C.** To date events before the birth of Christ, we count backward. The numbers continue indefinitely, as they do in A.D. When counting years B.C., the lower the number, the later the event. For example, something that happened in 500 B.C. took place 10 years later than an event that occurred in 510 B.C.

A. Tell students that people have been exploring since they appeared on Earth. Create a time line using a roll of bathroom tissue to illustrate how little time our planet has been inhabited.

B. Hold the end of the tissue and let it roll out on the floor. Have students predict how many tissue squares represent the amount of time civilizations have existed. (The first square represents the time elapsed from the early cave dwellers of the Stone Age to today.)

C. Hold the tissue square in the air, still attached to the roll, and mark off approximately 1/16 of an inch. Have students predict the amount of time that 1/16 of an inch represents. (The amount of time that civilized people lived on Earth.)

D. Unroll the tissue all the way to illustrate the short period of time for civilization.

E. Ask students if they know the exact date civilization began. (No one knows for certain. That is why people sometimes use the small "c" in front of the year. That stands for the Latin word "**circa**" meaning "about.")

F. Ask students if they have ever seen a date with B.C. or A.D. Have them explain what it means using the Background Information.

Closure

A. Ask students to calculate the length of time represented by each sheet of bathroom tissue. If the dinosaurs roamed the Earth 250 million years ago and the roll has 500 sheets, how many years does each square represent? (500,000)

B. Have students compute the number of years represented by an inch, one-half of an inch, one-quarter of an inch, one-eighth of an inch, and one-sixteenth of an inch. (Answers: One inch = 100,000 years, half-inch = 50,000 years, quarter inch = 25,000 years, eighth of an inch = 12,500 years, and a sixteenth of an inch = 6,250 years.)

Extensions

A. Ask students to sequence the following dates from time most distant to present day:

8000 B.C.	1 B.C.	1 A.D.	2003 A.D.
500 B.C.	3000 B.C.	1500 A.D.	100 A.D.

Answer: 8000 B.C., 3000 B.C., 500 B.C., 1 B.C., 1 A.D., 100 A.D., 1500 A.D., 2003 A.D.

B. Have students create a time line of anything that started B.C. (transportation, communication, etc.)

Assessment

Check the Closure activity for accuracy.

Activity 11- Ancient Inventions

Differentiation Strategies

Knowledge and Skills
- Attributes
- Visualization

Multiple Perspectives
- Inquiry
- Transformation

Communication
- Uses Technological Media
- Research

Enduring Understanding
Perseverance may make previously impossible tasks a reality.

Guiding Questions
(F) What is the force called work?
(F) What are the types of simple machines?
(C) How do simple machines make work easier?

Instructional Materials
- computer with Internet access
- books about simple machines and dictionaries

Optional:
- *How Do You Lift a Lion?* book, by Robert E. Wells

Background Information

Work, scientifically speaking, happens when someone or something causes another thing to move. Work is considered to be a push, pull, or lift.

Humans have always sought to make work easier. Most early inventions were created out of necessity. It would have been impossible for slaves to carry the large stones that built the towering pyramids. The ancient cultures had to devise ways to lift and move these enormous stones.

Simple machines are the basic components of items that have moving parts today. There are six simple machines: lever, pulley, wheel and axle, inclined plane, wedge, and gears. Every machine with moving parts, such as cars, printers, and ceiling fans, are based on simple machines invented centuries ago.

Simple machines give the user a **mechanical advantage** over the object being moved.

A. Share the Background Information. Have students form six teams. Provide each team a dictionary and have them look up the definition of one of the simple machines. Invite each team report the definition. Record definitions on the chalkboard.

B. Challenge teams to create a graphic organizer with the simple machines listing examples of how they are used under each heading. Here is a sample to get them started:

lever	pulley	inclined plane	wheel and axle	wedge	gears
wheelbarrow broom nutcracker scissors	flagpole crane blinds elevator	ramp screw stairs escalator	wagon bicycle vacuum skates	doorstop ax	watch bicycle car

C. Ask each team to learn as much as possible about one simple machine. Encourage teams to use the following Web site. As always, please preview all sites before allowing student access.
http://sln.fi.edu/qa97/spotlight3/spotlight3.html

D. Have students create presentations (using the rubric on Attachment 8 as a guide) that include the following information and visuals:
- special vocabulary about the simple machine (i.e., load, fulcrum, etc.)
- information about the origins of the simple machine
- ways the simple machine has evolved
- ways the simple machine is used in mechanical devices today
- a working model of the simple machine that demonstrates how it makes work easier

E. Invite students to share their presentations with the class.

Closure
Ask students to consider what the world would be like if simple machines had never been developed. Discuss the problems of work without simple machines.

Extensions
A. Encourage students to create a classroom Web site about simple machines. The Web site should contain each team's research in published form and pictures of the models.

B. Have students simplify their presentations to teach younger students. Provide a copy of *How Do You Lift a Lion?* around which students can build a simple machines lesson. Instruct students to ask for permission to teach the lesson to classes of younger students.

C. Invite students to explore the following Web site. It allows students to attempt to balance a simple lever with five different weights. As always, please preview all sites before allowing student access.
http://www.studyworksonline.com/cda/content/applet/0,,NAV2-96_SAP1703,00.shtml

Assessment
Use the rubric on Attachment 8 to evaluate the product and presentation from Step E.

Activity 12 - Exploring the Impossible

Differentiation Strategies

Knowledge and Skills
- Visualization
- Transformation

Analysis and Synthesis
- Convergent and Divergent Thinking
- Problem Defining

Multiple Perspectives
- Shared Inquiry
- Evaluate Situations

Methodology and Use of Resources
- Uses Technological Media
- Research

Enduring Understanding
Perseverance may make previously impossible tasks a reality.

Guiding Questions
(F) What is perseverance?
(F) What accomplishments were once believed impossible?
(C) How have the achievements of explorers who persevered to accomplish the impossible changed our reality?

Instructional Materials
- books about exploring the bottom of the ocean, climbing Mount Everest, traveling to the north and south poles, going to the moon, etc.
- computer with Internet access

Background Information

For centuries humans stared at the sky and the birds and wished they could fly. Greek **mythology** contains stories of the sun god flying across the sky each day. People were always curious about flying. But not until the Wright brothers invented the airplane did we get our feet off the ground.

People wondered what was at the bottom of the sea for ages. Now technology has advanced so that special submarines can take scientists to the deepest parts of the ocean to study the final frontier on Earth.

People stared up at the moon for centuries and wondered if man would ever set foot there. On July 20, 1969, a man on the moon became a reality.

All of these things at one time or another were considered impossible. Yet, through **perseverance** and hard work, each fantastic feat was achieved. What are the impossibilities of today? Exploring Mars? Traveling to the edge of the solar system?

A. Challenge students to imagine life in the 1800s. In those times, people in the cities worked in factories and lived in apartments. Conditions were poor for the hardworking people. People living on the frontier had the problems of growing their own food and having enough people to do all the work. Have students elaborate on these perspectives.

B. Next have students imagine two men in North Carolina trying to build a machine that would allow people to fly. Ask students to consider what people must have thought about the flying machine and its designers. Did people really think the machine would fly?

C. Have students brainstorm other impossibilities that have occurred over the past 100 years. Share the Background Information. Ask students to brainstorm the impossibilities of today.

D. Encourage students to select an impossibility from the past or the present to research. Below are a few suggested topics and Web sites. As always, please preview all sites before allowing student access.
- Climbing Mount Everest
http://www.asahi-net.or.jp/~nm3k-tgc/mountain/everest.html
- Exploring the north and south poles
http://unmuseum.mus.pa.us/henson.htm
- Exploring Mars
http://mars.jpl.nasa.gov/
- Exploring the ocean floor
http://www.divediscover.whoi.edu/cruise5/index.html

E. Have students prepare a creative presentation (using the rubric on Attachment 8 or one they create as a guide) to showcase their research. Presentations should include the following information:
- Time line of the history surrounding the impossible task
- famous explorers and researchers associated with the task
- current work on the task, or work being done as the result of the task
- ethical problems associated with the completion of the task (for example, for people to travel to Mars at present, it would take many years)
- the effects of the task being completed

Closure
Invite students to share their presentations with the class. Encourage the audience to take notes and ask questions after the presentations.

Extensions
A. Encourage students to research the possibility of completing a task that is considered impossible. Have students discover what steps will have to be taken for the impossibility to become a reality.

B. Give each student a piece of paper and tell them to fold it into a paper airplane. Have them write their names on the plane and on the count of 3 tell students to throw their planes to the front of the classroom. Once they have been thrown ask the following questions:

- Which one went the farthest? Why?
- Was it the plane design? If so, why?
- Was it the 'pilot'? If so, why?
- How can we experiment to discover which was better, the plane or the 'pilot'?

Have students discuss the options and introduce the ideas of control groups and variables. If students choose to use only one pilot they are controlling one variable. If students choose to use only one plane they are controlling one variable in the experiment.

Assessment
Assess student reports using the rubric that was selected.

Notes

Activity 13 – The Greatest Explorers

Differentiation Strategies
Ethics/Unanswered Questions
- Provocative Questions
- Inquiry

Multiple Perspectives
- Shared Inquiry
- Point of View

Communication
- Research
- Writing Skills

Relevance and Significance
- Role Playing
- Simulation

Enduring Understanding
Accomplishing previously impossible tasks may encourage future explorers to take a calculated risk.

Guiding Questions
(F) Who were some of the greatest explorers?
(C) How did the contributions of great explorers affect society?

Instructional Materials
- biographies and other resource books about famous explorers such as Lewis and Clark, Columbus, Zengh Ho, Sir Douglas Mawson, Captain Cook, Pedro de Alvarado, etc.
- computer with Internet access
- paper plates
- tongue depressors or craft sticks
- Copies of Attachment 14

Optional:
- props for a play

A. Invite students to research a famous explorer using biographies and research materials from the library.

B. As each student completes the reading assignment, distribute copies of the Explorers Tic-Tac-Toe on Attachment 14.

C. After students complete the Tic-Tac-Toe, have each child make a simple mask (on a paper plate mounted on a tongue depressor) that represents the person about whom he or she read.

Closure

Have each student pretend to be a famous explorer, reading or talking through the mask to explain his or her adventure. Before students begin the project have them develop a scoring rubric using the blank rubric on Attachment 3.

Extensions

A. Have the class vote on the explorer they feel has had the most influence on the world.

B. Students can write a play about a famous **expedition** made by one or more of the explorers. Create music or ask the music teacher for suggestions, make or gather simple props and costumes, and locate a stage area to perform the play. Allow students to practice the play several times. Have students make posters advertising the play. Invite students from other classes to see the play. Encourage students to invite their parents to a special evening performance.

C. Ask students to create a **budget** for the play and calculate how many tickets they would need to sell and at what price they would need to sell them to cover their expenses. This can be hypothetical as there should be no need to charge admission.

D. Invite students to visit, an interactive Web site that follows the journey of Lewis and Clark through the decisions of the student. As always, please preview all sites before allowing student access.
http://www.nationalgeographic.com/features/97/west/

Assessment

Evaluate the presentation made during Closure using the rubric that was created.

Notes

_____
_____
_____
_____
_____
_____
_____
_____
_____
_____

Activity 14 – Winter Survival

Differentiation Strategies

Knowledge and Skills
- Demonstration
- Draw Conclusions

Analysis and Synthesis
- Evaluate Situations
- Creative Problem Solving

Multiple Perspectives
- Shared Inquiry
- Point of View

Methodology and Use of Resources
- Inquiry
- Research

Enduring Understanding
Accomplishing previously impossible tasks may encourage future explorers to take a calculated risk.

Guiding Questions
(F) What are the three basic needs for survival?
(C) How does Brian accomplish his survival needs?
(C) Why would an all meat diet be lacking in nutrition?

Instructional Materials
- matching multiple copies of *Brian's Winter* book, by Gary Paulsen
- journals

Background Information
Gary Paulsen has written hundreds of books and has won the Newbery Honor Award three times. He has held a variety of jobs, and his diverse background helps him write books and short stories. His books about winter survival were based on his own survival during two runnings of the **Iditarod**, an Alaskan dog sled race that covers 1,180 miles. He wrote *Brian's Winter* as a sequel to *Hatchet* after fan mail asked, "What if Brian hadn't been rescued at the end of summer? What would have happened then?"

A. Decide how you will handle reading *Brian's Winter*. Will students read it in class or outside class? Before allowing students to read the book, ask them to brainstorm things a person would need to survive a harsh winter in the wilderness.

B. As students read the book, challenge them to keep a diary of the days Brian is stranded. Ask them to write from Brian's point of view.

C. After reading the first three chapters, have students research Native American bows and arrows. Encourage students to fashion bows and arrows and demonstrate their use.

D. Have students build model shelters similar to the one Brian had. Have students discuss construction, insulation, and heating after they have constructed the shelters.

E. Invite students to research the problems associated with eating only meat. Have students research the vitamins and minerals that would be lacking in the diet, as well as the toll the lack of these vitamins can take on the body.

F. Have students research the climate in Canada during winter. Then have students research the climate in your area in winter. Ask students to compare the two climates and determine the needs to survive the winter in your climate.

G. Have students work with a small group to complete the six hat thinking activity on Attachment 15.

H. After reading *Brian's Winter*, have students read *Hatchet*. Ask students to compare Brian's character in both books and determine whether Paulsen remained true to Brian's original character from *Hatchet*. Have students cite examples to prove their positions.

> **Teacher Tip**
> Six Thinking Hats-created by
> **Dr. De Bono** in the 1980s.
> White Hat – Facts
> Red Hat – Feeling and emotions
> Black Hat – Judgment and caution
> Yellow Hat – Logical Positive
> Green Hat – Creativity
> Blue Hat – Process Control

Closure

Have students write reviews of the book based on readability, enjoyment, whether the story was realistic, and what Paulsen could have done to make the book more enjoyable. Go over the Rubric on Attachment 8 so students will know what the expectations are for the review.

Extensions

A. *Brian's Winter* is the second book in a trilogy. Invite students to read the third book, *Brian's Return*. Ask students to evaluate all three books and write essays telling which was their favorite and why.

B. Have students record the daily highs and lows through the winter months. Graph these temperatures on a line graph and compare the temperatures with the area where Brian was stranded in class. Have students collect highs and lows for different parts of the country and compare them to the local climate graphically.

Assessment

Evaluate the Closure activity using the rubric on Attachment 8.

Activity 15 - Exploring Energy

Differentiation Strategies
Knowledge and Skills
- Attributes
- Classifying

Analysis and Synthesis
- Creative Problem Solving
- Evaluate Situations

Communication
- Research
- Demonstration

Relevance and Significance
- Futuristics
- Resource Person

Instructional Materials
- chart paper
- computer with Internet access
- books and other resources about power and energy
- journals

Enduring Understanding
Exploring societal issues, such as hunger and energy sources, may promote solutions to these problems.

Guiding Questions
(F) What are fossil fuels?
(F) What are some examples of alternate forms of energy?

Background Information
The United States continually encounters problems because of its dependence on **fossil fuels** such as coal, oil, and natural gas as our main sources of **energy**. If **alternative** sources of power do not become more available, power **outages** and **rationing** may become regular events in our country.

During this activity, students will learn about sources of power used today and possible sources for the future. Teams will research a form of energy, create a visual (the paper pyramid on Attachment 16 would be a suggestion), and present their findings.

A. Ask students to brainstorm many kinds of power or energy. Record responses on chart paper. Inform students they are beginning a study of energy. Initiate a discussion about the availability of fossil fuels for the future.

B. Have students go to the following Web site. It is an excellent, student-friendly resource. It provides descriptions of several forms of energy, such as **geothermal**, **nuclear**, fossil fuels, **hydroelectric**, **solar**, ocean, and wind. As always, please preview all sites before students view them.
http://www.energyquest.ca.gov/index.html

Several links at the following Web site will allow students to learn more about the types of energy we use today and the alternatives for tomorrow.
http://www.eia.doe.gov/kids/onlineresources.html

C. Have students form seven teams. Each should select a form of power to research.

D. Ask students to use the following research guidelines:
- Identify the source of power
- Explain how it was created or came about
- Tell where it is used or where it will be used in the future
- Name a pioneer in this field of power (if applicable)
- Explain how this form of power can help us in the future

> **Teacher Tip**
> Invite a representative from your local power company to come in and share information, concerns and possible solutions to the current energy needs of our country. Find out how your region differs from that of other areas around the country.

E. Instruct students to write an informative report about the energy source. The report should be planned using pre-writing strategies, edited, and printed on a word processor.

F. Have students create visuals to accompany their presentations. The visuals can be in the form of a demonstration, experiment, diagram, or illustration.

G. Invite groups to present their findings.

Closure
Encourage students to discuss our energy crisis and the solutions being explored and proposed.

Extensions
A. Have students help plan and design a Web site highlighting student research on power and energy. They should create a site map on paper showing links in the site. Take digital pictures of the visuals to include with the text.

B. When the site is running, have students write to their representatives in Congress and to the President of the United States, voicing their concerns about the energy crisis in America. Have students refer these politicians to the Web site they created. Students can look up their representatives in the U.S. House of Representatives and Senate at the below Web sites. Traditional mail addresses are also available at these sites.
http://www.house.gov/writerep/
http://www.senate.gov/general/contact_information/senators_cfm.cfm
http://www.congress.org/congressorg/home/

C. Ask students to bring in a copy of their home electric, gas or power bill. Examine the monthly quantity of power used. Calculate the daily usage and hourly usage of this power. Have students discuss ways to cut the amount of power usage in their own homes.

Assessment
Assess reports and visuals using the rubric on Attachment 8.

Notes

Activity 16 – Geometric Explorations

Differentiation Strategies
Knowledge and Skills
- Attributes
- Aesthetic thinking

Analysis and Synthesis
- Creative Problem Solving
- Evaluation

Communication
- Demonstration
- Research

Enduring Understanding
Explorers may transfer parts of their culture to other cultures.

Guiding Questions
(F) What are tessellations?
(C) How do patterns differ between countries?
(C) Why did people create tessellations?

Instructional Materials
- computer with Internet access

Optional:
- *The Magic of M.C. Escher* book, by M.C. Escher et al.
- books containing famous architecture

Background Information
Tessellations are repeating patterns of the same shape locked together. Everyday examples of simple tessellations might be found on tile floors, patterns on linoleum, shower curtain patterns, and bedspread patterns.

M.C. Escher is known for his study and brilliance in creating tessellations, but the technique has been around for centuries. Tessellations have been used to solve math problems, to decorate palace walls, to create dramatic rugs, and in clothing design. One can also find tessellations in nature.

This exploration of tessellations will give students the opportunity to examine tessellations, their history, and some of the more famous examples of tessellations used in architecture dating to the 12th century.

A. Share the first two paragraphs of the Background Information. Then direct students to the following Web site to discover more about tessellations. As always, please preview all sites before allowing student access.
http://library.thinkquest.org/16661/history.html

B. Guide students through the four galleries, focusing on the historical content and the similarities and differences between tessellations from different cultures.

© Prufrock Press Inc.

C. Encourage students to record favorite tessellations, the time periods, and the cultures from which their tessellations derived.

D. If using *The Magic of M.C. Escher*, allow time for students to browse the book.

E. Challenge students to combine their favorite styles to create an original tessellation.

F. When students complete their tessellations, have them write an essay telling about the influence different time periods and different cultures had on their work.

Closure

A. Invite students to share tessellations and essays with the class. Have them mount and display their tessellations and essays on a bulletin board.

B. Ask students the following questions about tessellations.
- Did you notice any patterns in complexity between cultures? Cite references to explain your answer.
- Did patterns get continually more difficult through time? Cite references to explain your answer.
- Why do you think people created tessellations?

Extensions

A. Invite students to search through books containing famous palaces or museums. Challenge them to find tessellations in the decoration of these buildings. Have students determine whether the use of a particular pattern by an artist was trying to convey a message. For example, tessellations on a palace wall might be trying to convey the message that the palace and kingdom was strong.

B. Challenge students to design a tessellation that conveys a message by its use of color and shapes. Have students write descriptions and essays explaining how they created their tessellations.

C. Have students go to the following Web site to explore its interactive tessellations. As always, please preview all sites before allowing student access. Why are these three shapes used in the program? How does the number of colors affect the pattern? **http://www.shodor.org/interactivate/activities/tessellate/**

Assessment

Assess student-created tessellations and essays from the Closure activity using the rubric on Attachment 8. Assess the answers to the questions in step B of the Closure activity.

Activity 17- Post-Assessment

Differentiation Strategies

Knowledge and Skills
- Attributes
- Classifying

Innovation and Application
- Fluency
- Flexibility

Multiple Perspectives
- Shared Inquiry
- Brainstorming

Instructional Materials
- journals

A. Challenge students to develop a word map with the word *Explorations* written in the middle. Tell students to create broad categories around the center word and then write specific examples under each category. This activity should be completed individually.

B. After 20 minutes, invite students to share their word maps.

C. Compare student word maps to the original brainstormed lists from the Pre-Assessment in Activity 1.

Notes

Instructional Materials
- 1 large sheet of construction paper per student
- 30 sheets of paper (lined or unlined) per student
- hole punch
- yarn

Instructions

1. Fold a large sheet of construction paper in half, like a book.

2. Create a journal cover, then glue it onto the front page of the construction paper book.

3. Place 30 pages of paper inside the construction paper book. Stack the edges evenly against the fold. Close the notebook.

4. Holding the paper tightly so it doesn't slide, make 3 hole punches along the bind. Loop each hole with a piece of yarn. Knot and tie in a bow.

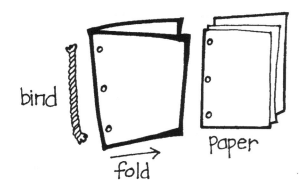

Journal 2

Instructional Materials
- 10 large pieces of construction paper per student (assorted colors)
- 30 pieces of paper (lines or unlined) per student
- hole punch
- stapler
- yarn

Instructions
1. Place a piece of construction paper on the table. Fold a pocket and staple the sides.

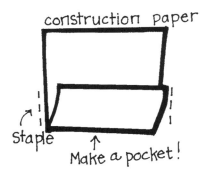

2. Add pieces of white paper

3. Punch holes and bind with yarn or string.

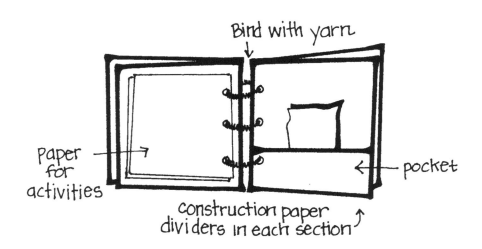

Attachment 2   Time Traveling Logic Problem

Use the matrix to help you find out when Marco Polo was in Rome. After you read a clue and determine the answer, put an "X" in the appropriate box.

	Fall	Winter	Spring	Summer
Ancient Egypt				
Ancient China				
Ancient Greece				
Ancient Rome				

Clues:

Marco Polo went to ancient China for the Chinese New Year. (February)

He went to Greece for the summer Olympics.

He climbed a pyramid in May.

When was Polo in Rome?

Student or Group: _____

Assignment: _____

Criteria	0 Working on It!	1 Novice	2 Acceptable	3 Out of the Box!

Comments

SCULPTURE

SCHOOLS

BOXING

POSTAL SYSTEM

GEOMETRY

JEWELRY

PEARS

COINS

WHEEL

LAW

MATH

BOWLING

CHECKERS

COMEDY

INK

DICE

CIRCUS

OLYMPICS

HOT-AIR BALLOON

FISHING REEL

PLAYING CARDS

COMPASS

CROSS BOW

PARACHUTES

SWORDS

KITES

CHESS

DYE

CONCRETE

YOGA

KARATE

NEWSPAPER

MONEY

ACROBATICS

WHEELBARROW

BRIDGES

STOP SIGNS

MEDICINE

GOVERNMENT

FOOTBALL

ACTING

COMEDY

FABLES

ARCHITECTURE

ROADS

COTTON

TOILETS

CALENDAR

CLARINET

MAKEUP

CITIES

BREAD

PAPER

WRITING

Ancient civilizations gave us many lasting gifts from their culture. Use the matrix to help you solve the puzzle.

	wheel	Olympics	tame cats	silk	architecture	yoga
The Fertile Crescent						
Ancient Egypt						
Ancient China						
Ancient India						
Ancient Greece						
Ancient Rome						

The Egyptians gave us a tame house pet.
The Chinese gave us beautiful, soft fabric made by worms.
A form of exercise and meditation originated in ancient India.
The Romans made a lot of contributions to building methods.
The Greeks took great pride in their athletes.
This means we can thank the ancient people of the Fertile Crescent for

_____.

☺I have jacks.
Who has the gift that helps us get around, move heavy objects and sometimes has spokes, and was given to us by the people of the earliest civilization?

I have wheel.

Who has the gift that involves athletes from many countries, and was originally started to honor Zeus, and was given to us by the people of Greece?

I have Olympics.

Who has a furry animal that is a popular pet, was domesticated, tamed, and worshipped by Egyptians?

I have cat.

Who has a study of math that involves shapes, lines, and angles, and was first written about by a Greek?

I have geometry?

Who has a gift that is a delicate fabric spun from worms and made only in China for many years?

I have silk.

Who has the Roman gift that I am using now in order to write this question?

I have the Roman alphabet.

Who has a gift that is a popular sport today using discipline, kicking, bowing, and originated in India?

I have karate.

Who has a popular fabric that most people wear to keep cool? It was first woven into fabric in India.

I have cotton.

Who has a gift that is a beautiful high-flying toy given to us by the Chinese?

I have kite.

Who has the Roman architectural design gift that is stronger than a beam and columns?

I have arch

Who has the gift of fruit from ancient history that can be eaten like an apple and is used to describe the shape of some things?

A have pear.

Who has the gift from Egypt that is a multi-million dollar business today and more popular with women then with men?

I have cosmetics or make up.

Who has the religion originating in India and one of the largest world religions today?

I have Buddhism.

Who has an invention from the Chinese that scouts and hikers usually carry with them in the woods and on trails?

I have compass.

Who has the gift from a Greek slave who wrote stories with morals or lessons, usually using animals?

I have Aesop's Fables.

Who has the woven material that was first used in the Fertile Crescent and comes from a goat?

I have mohair.

Who has a form of exercise that relaxes you and started in India?

I have yoga.

Who has the architectural design created by the Greeks? Ionic, Doric, and Corinthian are good clues.

I have column.

Who has the gift that was originally played with the knucklebones of sheep and originated in biblical times?

Attachment 7   Generalization Rubric

Student or Team: _____

Assignment: _____

Directions: Mark the appropriate rating for each criterion. Use these individual ratings to assign an overall rating for the assignment.

RATINGS	0 Working on it!	1 Novice	2 Acceptable	3 Out of the Box!
Generalizations	Unable to make a generalization with help	Began to make generalizations between ideas with help	Made simple generalizations with little help	Made complex generalizations between ideas with no help

Extended Skills to Consider:
- making generalizations between two or more disciplines
- extending to apply generalizations to other real-world problems

Comments:

Attachment 8 — Evaluation Rubric

Student or Team: _____

Assignment: _____

Directions: Mark the appropriate rating for each criterion. Use these individual ratings to assign an overall rating for the assignment.

Criteria	0 Working on it!	1 Novice	2 Acceptable	3 Out of the Box!	Not Applicable
Uses Pre-writing strategies	Cannot generate pre-writing graphic organizers, notes, or brain-storming	Some use of pre-writing in the form of organizers, notes, or brainstorming	Use of more than one pre-writing strategy; mostly well organized and thought out	Numerous strategies used and followed to create a well-organized and thought-out composition	N/A
Content is valid and accurate	Content is weak and shows little insight	Content is accurate but lacks insight; few supporting examples	Content is accurate with some questions left unanswered and a few supporting examples	Content is 100 percent accurate and has supporting examples	N/A
Organization	Not organized	Somewhat organized	Very organized	Organization far exceeded the standards	N/A
Oral Presentation of information	Could not express or present information	Presentation lacked creativity and was not very informative	Presentation moderately creative, entertaining, and informative	Engaging presentation that was creative, entertaining, and informative	N/A
OVERALL					

Comments:

The **scientific method** is a process developed by scientists to learn more about the world. In simplest terms, the scientific method is all about asking questions, observing, making guesses, testing guesses, and trying to develop theories.

There are four main steps in the scientific method. **Observation** is the first step. When we observe something, we use our five senses to make sense of it. During this step, scientists ask many questions about what they are observing. An example would be a scientist observing water beads on the outside of a glass. The question might be, "Why is water on the outside of the glass?"

The next step in the scientific method is to develop a **hypothesis**. A hypothesis is a possible explanation for the observation. There may be many hypotheses for one observation. In the example above, a hypothesis might be that the glass was leaking or got wet when water sprayed on it.

The third step in the scientific method is **prediction**. Scientists develop testable predictions about their hypotheses. Testable means scientists can create an experiment to test the hypothesis. In the example above, the scientist might develop a test in which he or she would dry the glass and fill it again to observe whether it would leak again.

The final step in the scientific method is to perform the **experiment**. An experiment helps prove or disprove the hypothesis. In the wet glass experiment, if a scientist discovers that water does not leak through the glass, he or she would choose another hypothesis. Then the scientist would again develop another testable prediction and perform an experiment to test the hypothesis.

When a scientist develops a hypothesis, makes a testable prediction, performs an experiment, and discovers that the hypothesis is correct, he or she must repeat the experiment many times. If the experiment produces the same results each time, then the hypothesis becomes a **theory**. A theory is a hypothesis that has been proven many times by many scientists.

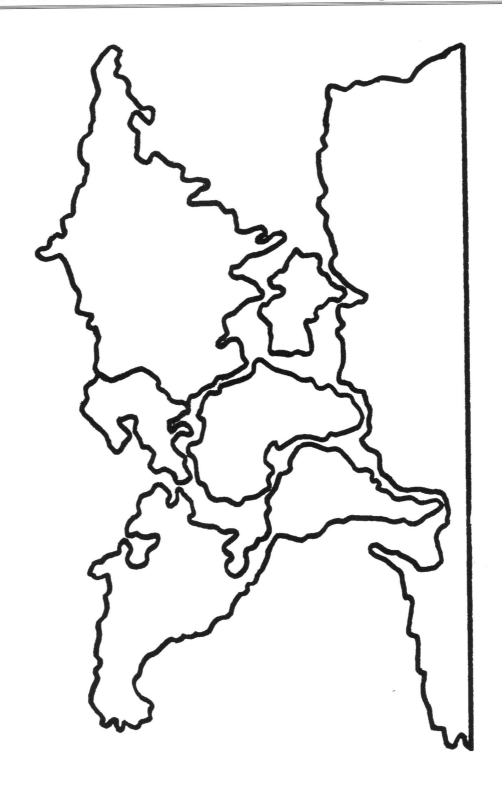

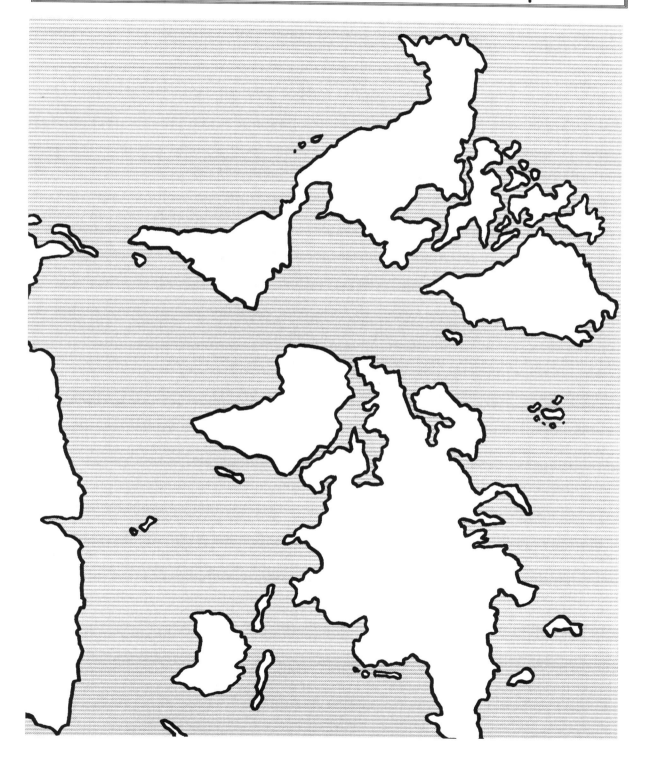

Reptiles Uncovered

By Al I. Gator
Scientists have found fossils of reptiles on the southwest coast of Africa. The amazing thing is, fossils from the same kinds of reptiles were found on the east coast of South America.

These discoveries have made scientists ask, "How did the same animals live on two continents so far away such a long time ago." Scientists are puzzled by their findings.

Fossilized Ferns Found

By Ima Plant
Children playing recently on the coast of Brazil discovered fossils of ferns that lived thousands of years ago. The children took the fossils home. The father of one child is a geologist, and he took the fossils to his lab for testing.

After testing, the lab discovered that the same kinds of ferns also lived off the coast of Africa. Scientists all over the world are wondering how this could happen.

Coal, Dinosaurs Discovered

By Ann Artica
Scientists in Antarctica have discovered coal deep beneath the polar ice cap. They were digging in the ice to see what they could find when they hit the coal.

This may not seem strange to us, but scientist Uma Reengold explains: "We know that coal forms in warm, wet areas. Coal is made from leaves and plants that have died, rotted, and decayed on the ground. As the rotten plants sink into the ground, the ground on top of it becomes heavier and heavier. The rotten plants eventually turn into coal from the weight of the ground above."

Scientists are puzzled about this discovery. They say the coal could not have formed near the polar area because it is too cold and dry.

Another exciting event occurred recently in Antarctica when dinosaur fossils were discovered. Scientists believe dinosaurs were cold-blooded reptiles that lived in warm, wet places. The discovery of fossilized dinosaur bones has scientists stumped.

Attachment 13   Brochure Evaluation

Student or Team:_____

Assignment: _____

Directions: Mark the appropriate rating for each criterion. Use these individual ratings to assign an overall rating for the assignment.

Criteria	0 Working on it!	1 Novice	2 Acceptable	3 Out of the Box!	Not Applicable
Visual Creativity and Appeal	Brochure is not well organized and lacks neatness	Brochure is somewhat organized and neatly illustrated	Brochure is organized and neatly illustrated	Brochure is published on the computer with many details and illustrations that support and expand upon the text	N/A
Content is valid and accurate	Content is weak and shows little insight	Content is accurate but lacks insight; few supporting examples	Content is accurate with some questions left unanswered and a few supporting examples	Content is 100 percent accurate and has supporting examples	N/A
Organization	Not organized	Somewhat organized	Very organized	Organization far exceeded the standards	N/A
Oral Presentation of information	Could not express or present information	Presentation lacked creativity and was not very informative	Presentation moderately creative, entertaining, and informative	Engaging presentation that was creative, entertaining, and informative	N/A
OVERALL					

Comments:

Read a biography or research a famous explorer. Then complete a tic-tac-toe in any direction by completing three of these activities during independent study. Lightly shade in the boxes as you complete each task.

Write	**Model**	**Math**
Write a report about the explorer. What important contributions did this explorer make to society?	Make a diorama to show the major contribution this person made during his or her exploration.	Collect at least ten numeric facts about your famous explorer. For example: date of birth, country of birth, number of expeditions, etc.
Survey Take a survey of opinions on an interesting question related to this person. For example: On a scale from one to ten, how important do you think the discovery was that your person is known for?	**Portrait** Draw a portrait of this famous explorer.	**Compare** Compare the person you read about to another famous explorer. Look for ways they are alike or different.
Fact File Collect interesting facts about the person about whom you are learning. Decide how many facts you want to collect and how you will display them.	**Research** List ten facts about the time in history that your famous explorer lived. Share what you find out with the group in an interesting way.	**Teach** Prepare and teach a lesson about this explorer.

Directions: Analyze Brian's wilderness survival using DeBono's Six Thinking Hats.

WHITE HAT

List three facts you learned about surviving in the Canadian wilderness during winter:

1.

2.

3.

BLACK HAT

What emotional problems and feelings did Brian continually fight while trying to survive?

RED HAT

How does Brian feel about killing animals? What was the alternative?

List the steps Brian used preparing for the winter.

BLUE HAT

What one thing would you have done differently if you had been there in Brian's place? What was the most creative use of a material that Brian created?

GREEN HAT

What did Brian learn about himself during this ordeal that could help him in the future?

YELLOW HAT

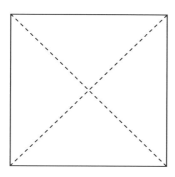

1. Begin with a square piece of paper.

2. Fold the square in half as shown, creating 2 creases.

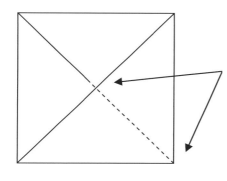

3. Unfold the square and cut from one corner to the center fold.

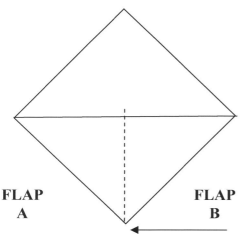

FLAP
A

FLAP
B

4. Fold Flap B under Flap A to create a three-dimensional triangular pyramid. Secure with glue or tape.

5. You can create a four-sided pyramid by making 4 paper pyramids and gluing the backsides together.

Explorations
Vocabulary and Materials Checklist

Activity	Vocabulary	Materials Needed
1		5 blank transparencies overhead projector 5 dry-erase markers journals or notebooks
2	mission Eastern Hemisphere	multiple matching copies of *Marco Polo: A Journey Through China* book, by Fiona MacDonald atlas and/or globe butcher paper, construction paper, and markers copies of Attachment 2
3	culture civilized civilization	journals computer with Internet access
4	cultural borrowing etymology	1 copy of Attachment 4 6 copies of Attachment 5 1 copy of Attachment 6 index cards tape
5	ancient Galileo Robert Goddard satellite	computer with Internet access books about space exploration
6	climatology continental drift meteorology Pangaea revolution supercontinent	3 copies of Attachment 9 (Scientific Method) 3 copies of Attachment 10 (Pangaea Jigsaw) 3 copies of Attachment 11 (World Map) 3 copies of Attachment 12 (News Flash!) computer with Internet access
7	submersibles	computer with Internet access books about ocean floor exploration
8	circulatory digestive excretory muscular nervous respiratory skeletal system	books about the human body computer with Internet access
9	Third World	computer with Internet access

	Emerging Nation	
10	A.D. B.C. circa	1 roll of toilet tissue marker
11	mechanical advantage simple machines work	computer with Internet access books about simple machines and dictionaries **Optional:** *How Do You Lift a Lion?* book, by Robert E. Wells
12	mythology perseverance	books about exploring the bottom of the ocean, climbing Mount Everest, traveling to the north and south poles, going to the moon, etc. computer with Internet access
13	expedition budget	biographies about famous explorers such as Lewis and Clark, Columbus, Zengh Ho, Sir Douglas Mawson, Captain Cook, Pedro de Alvarado, etc. computer with Internet access paper plates tongue depressors or craft sticks Copies of Attachment 14
14	Iditarod	matching multiple copies of *Brian's Winter* book, by Gary Paulsen journals
15	alternatives energy fossil fuels geothermal hydroelectric nuclear outages rationing solar	chart paper computer with Internet access books and other resources about power and energy journals
16	tessellations	computer with Internet access **Optional:** *The Magic of M.C. Escher* book, by M.C. Escher et al. books containing famous architecture
17		journals

Note: Paper and pencils should be on-hand each day, as should writing and illustration supplies, and may not be listed on the Checklist.

Explorations

Differentiation Strategies and TEKS Checklist

Activity	Differentiation Strategies	TEKS: Reading and Language Arts	TEKS: Mathematics	TEKS: Social Studies	TEKS: Science
1	**Knowledge and Skills** Attributes **Innovation and Application** Fluency **Multiple Perspectives** Brainstorming	Develop vocabulary by listening to selections read aloud			
2	**Knowledge and Skills** Visualization Research **Analysis and Synthesis** Evaluate Situations Draw Conclusions SCAMPER **Relevance and Significance** Field Lesson Group Consensus	Determine the purposes for listening such as to gain information Locate the meanings, pronunciations, and derivations of unfamiliar words using dictionaries, glossaries, and other sources Develop vocabulary by listening to selections read aloud Establish and adjust purposes for reading such as reading to find out, to understand, to interpret,		Apply geographic tools, including grid systems, legends, symbols, scales, and compass roses, to construct and interpret maps Identify the accomplishments of significant explorers Translate geographic data into a variety of formats such as raw data to graphs and maps	

Activity	Differentiation Strategies	TEKS: Reading and Language Arts	TEKS: Mathematics	TEKS: Social Studies	TEKS: Science
		to enjoy, and to solve problems Represent text information in different ways such as in outline, time line, or graphic organizer			
3	**Knowledge and Skills** Classifying Etymology **Innovation and Application** Flexibility Fluency **Multiple Perspectives** Shared inquiry Brainstorming	Determine the purposes for listening such as to gain information Locate the meanings, pronunciations, and derivations of unfamiliar words using dictionaries, glossaries, and other sources Develop vocabulary by listening to selections read aloud Establish and adjust purposes for reading such as reading to find out, to understand, to interpret, to enjoy, and to solve problems Represent text information in different ways such as in outline,	Relate informal language to mathematical language and symbols Identify the mathematics in everyday situations	Summarize the contributions of people of selected racial, ethnic, and religious groups to our national identify Identify the similarities and differences within and among selected racial, ethnic, and religious groups in the United States	

Activity	Differentiation Strategies	TEKS: Reading and Language Arts	TEKS: Mathematics	TEKS: Social Studies	TEKS: Science
		time line, or graphic organizer			
4	**Knowledge and Skills** Etymology Research **Innovation and Application** Logic Problems Fluency **Analysis and Synthesis** Generalizations Inferences	Draw inferences such as conclusions or generalizations and support them with text evidence and experience Develop vocabulary by listening to selections read aloud Offer observations, make connections, react, speculate, interpret, and raise questions in response to texts		Summarize the contributions of people of selected racial, ethnic, and religious groups to our national identify Identify the similarities and differences within and among selected racial, ethnic, and religious groups in the United States	
5	**Analysis and Synthesis** Creative Problem Solving Evaluate Situations **Ethics/Unanswered Questions** Provocative Questions **Multiple Perspectives** Shared Inquiry **Methodology and Use of Resources** Research	Establish and adjust purposes for reading such as reading to find out, to understand, to interpret, and to solve problems Draw inferences such as conclusions or generalizations and support them with text evidence and experience Draw conclusions from information gathered from multiple sources	Solve problems involving length, including time Relate informal language to mathematical language and symbols	Organize and interpret information in outlines, reports, databases, and visuals including graphs, charts, time lines, and maps Analyze information by sequencing, categorizing, identifying cause-and-effect relationships, comparing, contrasting, finding the main idea, summarizing, making generalizations and predictions, and drawing inferences and conclusions	Evaluate the impact of research on scientific thought, society, and the environment

Activity	Differentiation Strategies	TEKS: Reading and Language Arts	TEKS: Mathematics	TEKS: Social Studies	TEKS: Science
		Write to inform such as to explain, describe, report, and narrate			Plan and implement descriptive and simple experimental investigations including asking well-defined questions, formulating testable hypotheses, and selecting and using equipment and technology
	Knowledge and Skills Research	Write to express, discover, record, develop, reflect on ideas, and to problem solve	Identify the mathematics in everyday situations	Communicate in written, oral, and visual forms	
	Analysis and Synthesis Convergent and Divergent Thinking	Use multiple sources, including electronic texts, experts, and print resources, to locate and organize information	Use addition and subtraction to solve problems	Use problem-solving and decision-making skills	Collect information by observing and measuring
	Multiple Perspectives Evaluate Situations	Interpret important events and ideas gathered from maps, charts, graphics, video segments, or technology presentations	Select or develop an appropriate problem-solving strategy	Apply critical-thinking skills to organize and use information acquired from a variety of sources	Communicate valid conclusions
6	**Relevance and Significance** Field Lesson	Draw conclusions from information gathered from multiple sources		Identify different points of view about an issue or topic	Analyze, review, and critique scientific explanations, including hypotheses and theories, as to their strengths and weaknesses using scientific evidence and information
		Frame questions to direct research		Offer observations, make connections, react, speculate, interpret, and raise questions in response to texts	
				Create written and visual material such as journal entries, reports, graphic organizers, outlines, and bibliographies Organize and interpret information in outlines, reports, databases, and visuals including graphs, charts, time lines, and maps	

77

Activity	Differentiation Strategies	TEKS: Reading and Language Arts	TEKS: Mathematics	TEKS: Social Studies	TEKS: Science
7	**Knowledge and Skills** Research **Analysis and Synthesis** Evaluate Situations **Multiple Perspectives** Inquiry **Communication** Demonstration Writing Skills	Determine the purposes for listening such as to gain information, to solve problems, or to enjoy and appreciate Adjust reading rate based on purposes for reading Draw conclusions from information gathered from multiple sources Summarize and organize ideas gained from multiple sources in useful ways Write to inform and entertain such as to explain, describe, report, and narrate		Apply critical-thinking skills to organize and use information acquired from a variety of sources Offer observations, make connections, react, speculate, interpret, and raise questions in response to texts Organize and interpret information in outlines, reports, databases, and Create written and visuals including graphs, charts, time lines, and maps	Communicate valid conclusions Analyze, review, and critique scientific explanations, including hypotheses and theories, as to their strengths and weaknesses using scientific evidence and information
8	**Knowledge and Skills** Attributes **Multiple Perspectives** Brainstorming **Methodology and Use of Resources** Research Shared Inquiry	Draw inferences such as conclusions or generalizations and support them with text evidence and experience Summarize and organize information from multiple sources by taking notes, outlining ideas, or making charts	Identify the mathematics in everyday situations Use addition and subtraction to solve problems	Analyze information by sequencing, categorizing, identifying cause-and-effect relationships, comparing, contrasting, finding the main idea, summarizing, making generalizations and predictions, and drawing inferences and conclusions	Describe some cycles, structures, and process that are found in a simple system Describe some interactions that occur in a simple system

78

Activity	Differentiation Strategies	TEKS: Reading and Language Arts	TEKS: Mathematics	TEKS: Social Studies	TEKS: Science
		Write to inform such as to explain, describe, report, and narrate Frame questions to direct research			
9	**Analysis and Synthesis** Evaluate Situations **Ethics/Unanswered Questions** Provocative Questions **Multiple Perspectives** Brainstorming **Communication** Research	Connect his/her own experiences, information, insights, and ideas with those of others through speaking and listening Draw inferences such as conclusions or generalizations and support them with text evidence and experience Summarize and organize information from multiple sources by taking notes, outlining ideas, or making charts Write to influence such as to persuade, argue, and request Write to inform such as to explain, describe, report, and narrate	Identify the mathematics in everyday situations Use models to relate decimals to fractions	Analyze information by sequencing, categorizing, identifying cause-and-effect relationships, comparing, contrasting, finding the main idea, summarizing, making generalizations and predictions, and drawing inferences and conclusions Express ideas orally based on research and experiences Create written and visual materials such as journal entries, reports, graphic organizers, or outlines Use a problem-solving process to identify a problem, gather information, list and consider options, consider advantages and disadvantages	
10	**Knowledge and Skills** Attributes	Develop vocabulary by listening to selections	Use addition and subtraction to solve	Analyze information by sequencing, categorizing,	

© Prufrock Press Inc.

Activity	Differentiation Strategies	TEKS: Reading and Language Arts	TEKS: Mathematics	TEKS: Social Studies	TEKS: Science
	Analysis and Synthesis Evaluate Situations Group Consensus **Communication** Demonstration	read aloud	problems involving whole numbers Locate and name points on a number line using whole numbers Identify the mathematics in everyday situations Select or develop an appropriate problem-solving strategy, including drawing a picture, looking for a pattern, or systematic guessing and checking	identifying cause-and-effect relationships, comparing, contrasting, finding the main idea, summarizing, making generalization and predictions, and drawing inferences and conclusions Organize and interpret information in outlines, reports, databases, and visuals including time lines	
11	**Knowledge and Skills** Attributes Visualization **Multiple Perspectives** Inquiry **Communication** Uses Technological Media Research	Locate the meanings, pronunciations, and derivations of unfamiliar words using dictionaries, glossaries, and other sources Establish and adjust purposes for reading such as reading to find out, to understand, to interpret, to enjoy, and to solve problems Paraphrase and summarize text to recall, inform, and organize		Express ideas orally based on research and experiences Incorporate main and supporting ideas in verbal and written communication	Analyze and interpret information to construct reasonable explanations from direct and indirect evidence Communicate valid conclusions

Activity	Differentiation Strategies	TEKS: Reading and Language Arts	TEKS: Mathematics	TEKS: Social Studies	TEKS: Science
		ideas Write to inform such as to explain, describe, report, and narrate			
12	**Knowledge and Skills** Visualization **Analysis and Synthesis** Convergent and Divergent Thinking **Multiple Perspectives** Shares Inquiry **Methodology and Use of Resources** Research	Describe mental images that text descriptions evoke Draw inferences such as conclusions or generalizations and support them with text evidence and experience Distinguish fact from opinion Draw conclusions from information gathered from multiple sources Write to express, discover, record, develop, reflect on ideas, and to problem solve		Identify famous inventors and scientists and their contributions Predict how future scientific discoveries and technological innovations might affect life Express ideas orally based on research and experiences Create written and visual materials such as journal entries, reports, graphic organizers, and outlines	Analyze and interpret information to construct reasonable explanations from direct and indirect evidence Communicate valid conclusions
13	**Ethics/Unanswered Questions** Provocative Questions **Multiple Perspectives** Shared Inquiry **Communication**	Draw inferences such as conclusions or generalizations and support them with text evidence and experience Paraphrase and summarize text to recall,		Identify the accomplishments of significant explorers and explain their impact on America Incorporate main and supporting ideas in verbal	

81

Activity	Differentiation Strategies	TEKS: Reading and Language Arts	TEKS: Mathematics	TEKS: Social Studies	TEKS: Science
	Research Writing Skills **Relevance and Significance** Simulation	inform, and organize ideas Offer observations, make connections, react, speculate, interpret, and raise questions in response to texts Write to entertain such as to compose humorous poems or short stories Write to inform such as to explain, describe, report, and narrate		and written communication Express ideas orally based on research and experiences	
14	**Knowledge and Skills** Demonstration **Analysis and Synthesis** Evaluate Situations **Multiple Perspectives** Shared Inquiry **Methodology and Use of Resources** Research	Adjust reading rate based on purposes for reading Draw on experiences to bring meanings to words in context such as interpreting figurative language and multiple-meaning words Offer observations, make connections, react, speculate, interpret, and raise questions in response to texts Connect, compare, and		Analyze information by sequencing, categorizing, identifying cause-and-effect relationships, comparing, contrasting, finding the main idea, summarizing, making generalizations and predictions, and drawing inferences and conclusions Identify different points of view about an issue or topic	

82

© Prufrock Press Inc.

Activity	Differentiation Strategies	TEKS: Reading and Language Arts	TEKS: Mathematics	TEKS: Social Studies	TEKS: Science
		contrast ideas, themes, and issues across text			
		Write to express, discover, record, develop, reflect on ideas, and to problem solve			
15	**Knowledge and Skills** Attributes	Use multiple sources, including electronic texts, experts, and print resources, to locate information relevant to research questions		Analyze information by sequencing, categorizing, identifying, cause-and-effect relationships, comparing, contrasting, finding the main idea, summarizing, making generalizations and predictions, and drawing conclusions	Compare the effects of scientific discoveries and technological innovations that have influenced daily life in different periods in U.S. history
	Analysis and Synthesis Creative Problem Solving Evaluate Situations	Produce research projects and reports in effective formats using visuals to support meaning as appropriate		Organize and interpret information from outlines, reports, databases, and visuals including graphs, charts, time lines, and maps	Make inferences and draw conclusions about effects of human activity on Earth's renewable, non-renewable, and inexhaustible resources
	Communication Research	Draw conclusions from information gathered from multiple sources		Use a problem-solving process to identify a problem, gather information, list and consider options, consider advantages and disadvantages, choose and implement a solution, and evaluate the effectiveness of the solution	Construct graphs, tables, maps, and charts using tools, including computers to organize, examine, and evaluate data
		Generate ideas and plans for writing			Evaluate the impact of research on scientific thought, society, and the environment
		Develop drafts by categorizing ideas, organizing them into paragraphs, and blending paragraphs			Describe interactions within ecosystems
		Use available technology			

83

Activity	Differentiation Strategies	TEKS: Reading and Language Arts	TEKS: Mathematics	TEKS: Social Studies	TEKS: Science
		to support aspects of creating, revising, editing, and publishing Proofread his/her own writing and that of others Select and use reference materials and resources as needed for writing, revising, and editing final drafts			
16	**Knowledge and Skills** Attributes **Analysis and Synthesis** Creative Problem Solving **Communication** Demonstration Research	Find similarities and differences across texts Read for varied purposes such as to be informed or to be entertained Use your own knowledge and experience to comprehend Write to express, discover, record, develop, reflect on ideas, and to problem solve	Make generalizations based on observed patterns and relationships Generate geometric definitions using critical attributes	Express ideas orally based on research and experiences Analyze information by sequencing, categorizing, identifying cause-and-effect relationships, comparing, contrasting, finding the main idea, summarizing, making generalizations and predictions, and drawing inferences and conclusions	
17	**Knowledge and Skills** Attributes **Innovation and Application** Fluency				

84

© Prufrock Press Inc.

Activity	Differentiation Strategies	TEKS: Reading and Language Arts	TEKS: Mathematics	TEKS: Social Studies	TEKS: Science
	Multiple Perspectives Brainstorming				

Explorations
National Standards Checklist

Activity	Language Arts and Reading	Mathematics	Social Studies	Science
1	Uses prewriting strategies to plan written work Uses a variety of strategies to plan research Uses strategies to compile information into written reports or summaries Uses prior knowledge and experience to understand and respond to new information Contributes to group discussions			

Activity	Language Arts and Reading	Mathematics	Social Studies	Science
2	Writes in response to literature Uses multiple representations of information Reads aloud familiar stories, poems, and passages with fluency and expression Establishes a purpose for reading Listens to classmates and adults	Uses trial and error and the process of elimination to solve problems Understands how scale in maps and drawings shows relative size and distance	Knows the basic elements of maps and globes Interprets topography using aerial photos and maps Uses map grids to plot absolute location Knows the similarities and differences in characteristics of culture in different regions Understands how cultures differ in their use of similar environments and resources Understands calendar time in years, decades, and centuries Understands that specific individuals had a great impact on history	

Activity	Language Arts and Reading	Mathematics	Social Studies	Science
3	Writes in response to literature Uses multiple representations of information Reads aloud familiar stories, poems, and passages with fluency and expression Establishes a purpose for reading Listens to classmates and adults	Uses trial and error and the process of elimination to solve problems Understands how scale in maps and drawings shows relative size and distance	Knows the basic elements of maps and globes Interprets topography using aerial photos and maps Uses map grids to plot absolute location Knows the similarities and differences in characteristics of culture in different regions Understands how cultures differ in their use of similar environments and resources Understands calendar time in years, decades, and centuries Understands that specific individuals had a great impact on history	
4	Uses a variety of strategies to plan research Contributes to group discussions	Uses trial and error and the process of elimination to solve problems	Knows significant historical achievements of various cultures of the world	
5	Writes expository compositions Uses a variety of strategies to plan research Uses electronic media to gather	Adds, subtracts, multiplies, and divides whole numbers and decimals Uses specific strategies to estimate computations and to	Knows different methods used to measure distance Knows how to construct time lines in significant historical developments that mark at evenly	Knows that the Earth is one of several planets that orbit the Sun and that the Moon orbits the Earth Knows that the patterns of stars in the sky stay the same, although

Activity	Language Arts and Reading	Mathematics	Social Studies	Science
	information Uses strategies to compile information into written reports or summaries Makes basic oral presentations to class	check the reasonableness of computational results Understands relationships between measures Understands that measurement is not exact Understands how scale in maps and drawings shows relative size and distance Understands that the word "chance" refers to the likelihood of an event Uses basic sample spaces to describe and predict events	spaced intervals the years, decades, and centuries Knows how to interpret data presented in time lines Understands that specific individuals had a great impact on history Knows the different forms of transportation and their developments over time	they appear to slowly move from east to west across the sky nightly and different stars can be seen in different seasons Knows that planets look like stars, but over time they appear to wander among the constellations Knows that astronomical objects in space are massive in size and are separated from one another by vast distances Knows that telescopes magnify distant objects in the sky and dramatically increase the number of stars we can see

Activity	Language Arts and Reading	Mathematics	Social Studies	Science
6	Uses strategies to write for a variety of purposes Uses a variety of strategies to plan research Uses electronic media to gather information Makes basic oral presentations to class Understands techniques used to convey messages in visual media	Adds, subtracts, multiplies, and divides whole numbers and decimals Understands relationships between measures Understands that measurement is not exact Understands how scale in maps and drawings shows relative size and distance Understands that when predictions are based on what is known about the past, one must assume that conditions stay the same from the past event to the predicted future event	Geography Knows the basic elements of maps and globes Interprets topography using aerial photos and maps Uses map grids to plot absolute location Knows different methods used to measure distance	Knows how features on the Earth's surface are constantly changed by a combination of slow and rapid processes Knows that fossils provide evidence about the plants and animals that lived long ago and the nature of the environment at that time Knows that an object's motion can be described by tracing and measuring its position over time Knows that although people using scientific inquiry have learned much about the objects, events, and phenomena in nature, science is an ongoing process and will never be finished
7	Uses strategies to write for a variety of purposes Uses a variety of strategies to plan research Uses electronic media to gather information Makes basic oral presentations to class Understands techniques used to	Understands relationships between measures Understands that numbers and the operations performed on them can be used to describe things in the real world and predict what might occur	History Understands that specific individuals had a great impact on history	Knows that most of Earth's surface is covered by water, that most of that water is salt water in oceans and fresh water is found in rivers, lakes, underground sources, and glaciers Knows that people of all ages, backgrounds, and groups have made contributions to science and technology throughout history

Activity	Language Arts and Reading	Mathematics	Social Studies	Science
	convey messages in visual media			
8	Uses strategies to edit and publish written work Uses a variety of strategies to plan research Uses electronic media to gather information Knows the main formats and characteristics of familiar media			Knows that living organisms have distinct structures and body systems that serve specific functions in growth, survival, and reproduction Knows that behavior of individual organisms is influenced by internal cues and external cues, and that humans and other organisms have senses that help them to detect these cues Knows that the transfer of energy is essential to all living organisms
9	Uses prewriting strategies to plan written work Uses a variety of strategies to plan research Uses electronic media to gather information Makes basic oral presentations to class	Adds, subtracts, multiplies, and divides whole numbers and decimals Adds and subtracts simple fractions Organizes and displays data in simple bar graphs, pie charts, and line graphs	Civics Understands the importance of voluntarism as a characteristic of American society	
10	Responds to questions and comments Listens to classmates and adults	Adds, subtracts, multiplies, and divides whole numbers and decimals Adds and subtracts simple fractions	Geography Knows different methods used to measure distance History Knows how to construct time	

91

Activity	Language Arts and Reading	Mathematics	Social Studies	Science
		Uses basic sample spaces to describe and predict events	lines in significant historical developments that mark at evenly spaced intervals the years, decades, and centuries Knows how to interpret data presented in time lines	
11	Uses a variety of strategies to plan research Uses dictionaries to gather information for research topics Uses electronic media to gather information Makes basic oral presentations to class	Organizes and displays data in simple bar graphs, pie charts, and line graphs	History Knows about the development of the wheel and its early uses in ancient societies Understands the development and the influence of basic tools on work and behavior	
12	Uses electronic media to gather information Uses electronic media to gather information Uses strategies to compile information into written reports or summaries Uses reading skills and strategies to understand a variety of literary passages and texts Contributes to group discussion		History Knows how to interpret data presented in time lines Understands that specific individuals had a great impact on history Understands that specific ideas had an impact on history Understands the challenges and difficulties encountered by people in pioneer farming communities Knows about technological	

Activity	Language Arts and Reading	Mathematics	Social Studies	Science
	Makes basic oral presentations to class		inventions and developments that evolved during the 19th century and the influence of these changes on the lives of workers	
13	Uses strategies to write for a variety of purposes Writes narrative accounts, such as poems and stories Uses a variety of strategies to plan research Uses electronic media to gather information Makes basic oral presentations to class Understands basic elements of advertising in visual media		History Understands that specific individuals had a great impact on history Understands the interactions that occurred between the Native Americans or Hawaiians and the first European, African, and Asian-Pacific explorers and settlers in the state or region	

Activity	Language Arts and Reading	Mathematics	Social Studies	Science
14	Evaluates own and others' writing Establishes a purpose for reading Uses reading skills and strategies to understand a variety of literary passages and texts Contributes to group discussions		Geography Knows the physical components of Earth's atmosphere, lithosphere, hydrosphere, and biosphere	

Activity	Language Arts and Reading	Mathematics	Social Studies	Science
	Uses prewriting strategies to plan written work		Geography Knows the characteristics, location, and use of renewable resources, flow resources, and nonrenewable resources	Knows that heat is often produced as a byproduct when one form of energy is converted to another form
	Uses strategies to edit and publish written work			Knows that although people using scientific inquiry have learned much about the objects, events, and phenomena in nature, science is an ongoing process and will never be finished
	Writes personal letters		Knows how settlement patterns are influenced by the discovery and use of resources	
	Uses a variety of strategies to plan research			
	Uses electronic media to gather information		Knows the relationships between economic activities and resources	Knows that scientists and engineers often work in teams to accomplish a task
	Uses strategies to compile information into written reports or summaries		Civics Knows that the government was created by people who had the following beliefs: the government is established by and for the people, the people have the right to choose their representatives, and the people have the right to change their government and the constitution	
15	Makes basic oral presentations to class			
			Knows how people can participate in their state and local government, and understands why it is important that people participate in their state and local government	
			Knows the names of his/her legislators at the state and national levels and the names of his/her representatives in the executive branches of government at the national, state, and local levels	

95

Activity	Language Arts and Reading	Mathematics	Social Studies	Science
16	Uses prewriting strategies to plan written work Uses a variety of strategies to plan research Uses electronic media to gather information Makes basic oral presentations to class	Knows basic geometric language for describing and naming shapes Recognizes a wide variety of patterns and the rules that explain them Understands that the same pattern can be represented in different ways	History Knows how to view the past in terms of the norms and values of the time Understands that specific individuals had a great impact on history Knows significant historical achievements of various cultures of the world	
17	Uses prewriting strategies to plan written work Uses a variety of strategies to plan research Uses strategies to compile information into written reports or summaries Uses prior knowledge and experience to understand and respond to new information Contributes to group discussions			

96